CREATING
THE CONDITIONS TO
INVOLVE PUPILS
IN THEIR LEARNING

A HANDBOOK OF ACTIVITIES TO DEVELOP PUPILS' LEARNING CAPACITY

JOHN BERESFORD

David Fulton Publishers
London

David Fulton Publishers Ltd
The Chiswick Centre, 414 Chiswick High Road, London W4 5TF

www.fultonpublishers.co.uk

David Fulton Publishers is a division of Granada Learning Limited, part of the Granada Media group.

First published in Great Britain by David Fulton Publishers 2003
10 9 8 7 6 5 4 3 2 1

Note: The rights of John Beresford to be identified as the author of this work has been asserted by him in accordance with the Copyright, Designs and Patents Act 1988.

Copyright © John Beresford 2003

British Library Cataloguing in Publication Data
A catalogue record for this book is available from the British Library.

ISBN 1–84312–064–X

All rights reserved. No part of this publication may be reproduced, stored in a retrieval system or transmitted, in any form, or by any means, electronic, mechanical, photocopying, recording or otherwise, without the prior permission of the publishers.

Typeset by FiSH Books, London.
Printed and bound in Great Britain by Ashford Colour Press Limited, Gosport, Hants

Contents

Acknowledgements

Producing a book of activities that involve teachers and pupils requires a lot of support. I would like to thank David Fulton Publishers for the suggestion of the book. I am also indebted to David Hopkins, who has been a friend and colleague for a number of years, and who, in 1998, took on the role of taskmaster as my tutor for the PhD at Nottingham University on which the book is based. I thank him for his kind but critical support, and for the friendship that I hope has survived the pupil-tutor relationship.

I have been very fortunate in the colleagues with whom I have worked in IQEA. They read very much like the *Who's Who* of school improvement – as well as David, there have been Mel West, Mel Ainscow, Judy Sebba, Geoff Southworth, Michael Fielding, Paul Clarke and Alma Harris. My frequent use of 'we' in the text is not intended to be regal – more an acknowledgement of the debt I owe to their intelligence and perception.

I would also like to thank the teachers who have tried out many of the activities in this book, and to the pupils who have also taken part. Finally, I would like to thank my partner and colleague Hilary Stokes, who has plied me with encouragement, coffee and technical support, while remaining an extremely critical friend. I could not have written this without her.

John Beresford
Cambridge, August 2002

About the book

Who is the book for?

This book is intended for anyone who has responsibility for improving schools. The reform agenda of the current government would suggest that this embraces all members of our educational system, from directors of education to classroom learning assistants. It is my hope that the book will be of such general interest, although the activities described later are intended for teachers and their pupils.

What does the book do?

The book provides activities and ideas to help create the conditions to improve pupil learning by developing pupil learning capacity. All the activities described involve pupils in some way – pupils being observed at work, pupils being asked for their opinions in interviews or by questionnaire, pupils discussing matters of educational concern with their teachers. It would be perverse, in a book which suggests that pupils should have considerable input into how they are taught and how they learn, for it to be otherwise.

How should the book be used?

Schools will have pupils at different stages in the development of their learning capacity. Hence some of the activities outlined in the book may appear too trite for schools that have already focused on aspects of the pupil conditions, while some will appear too radical to schools where pupils' views on their learning are less regularly canvassed. For example, the section on school and classroom rules (Chapter 7) deals with issues that some teachers may find sensitive. It is hoped that teachers will choose activities that they deem appropriate to the learning capacity of their own pupils, in order that they can incrementally build the classroom and school culture that makes their pupils more effective learners, and that will make their schools more effective schools. It is also hoped that schools will adapt to their own requirements the ideas, instruments and schedules contained in the book.

How is the book organised?

The six pupil conditions described in the book have been identified both in working with schools and in a reinterpretation of the classroom conditions from the viewpoint of pupils. The first chapter explains this reinterpretation, and subsequent chapters elaborate on each of the conditions, as well as providing activities that contribute to building pupils' learning capacity. Chapter 8 outlines the changes in school and classroom culture which are the corollary of the book's focus on developing pupils' learning capacity.

Where do the ideas come from?

This book is based upon work carried out since 1995 on devising a research instrument to assess the views of pupils on how their learning is organised (Beresford 2002). This required a reconceptualisation of the IQEA (*Improving the Quality of Education for All*) classroom conditions into a form recognisable to pupils. In addition, each of the resulting pupil conditions has also been refined with reference to both fieldwork research within the project, and to the research of others working in a similar area.

Do I need to be an expert researcher to undertake these activities?

Nearly all of the activities described are small-scale, and are intended for use with classes or smaller teaching groups. They are designed to be simple but useful activities – simple, in that the information collected will not require painstaking analysis, and useful, because it is hoped they will provide information on how to improve the learning experiences of pupils. Where analysis is necessary, examples and easy-to-follow instructions have been provided. Many of the activities have been tried by teachers, and it is hoped that those trying them for the first time will adapt them to their own particular needs.

CHAPTER 1

IQEA, pupils and school improvement

Introduction

The IQEA (*Improving the Quality of Education for All*) project has recently celebrated its tenth birthday. During that decade the project has moved its base from Cambridge to Nottingham and now, partly because the academics on whom the project draws have dispersed to various universities, it has become a limited company. During those ten years, these colleagues have worked with upwards of 200 schools in at least four continents. As research officer to the project since 1994 I have had the pleasure of working with teachers in East Anglia, Humberside, Walsall, Peterborough, Leicester, Merthyr, Nottinghamshire, Derbyshire, Sunderland and Hong Kong.

The IQEA project arose from the need for schools to cope with the pressures of enforced change following the legislation of the late 1980s and early 1990s, and from the efforts of some Cambridge-based academics to help schools cope with these changes. That help was based on the premise that schools needed to develop their internal capacity to manage change, while pursuing their own reform agendas to provide quality education for their pupils. Early work with a small number of primary and secondary schools gave rise to a recognition that this capacity-building would involve most schools in a process of change in how they conducted their internal processes (Ainscow *et al.* 1994; Ainscow *et al.* 2000) and in how they conducted their professional relationships. In short, the change would in part need to be cultural.

From subsequent research within the project, it became clear that successful schools not only paid attention to internal management processes but also to what was happening in their classrooms. A set of classroom conditions was conceptualised (Hopkins *et al.* 1995; Hopkins *et al.* 1997; Hopkins *et al.* 1998). This conceptualisation arose from a combination of empirical research findings from within the IQEA project and a review of the literature of effective teaching and learning (Beresford 1995). Subsequent work within the project has explored ways in which teachers can develop their teaching repertoires (Hopkins and Harris 2000), the role of the school department in school improvement (Harris 2002) and how a school improvement project is organised (Hopkins 2002). There has also been a sample collection of research instruments that teachers could use in their school improvement programmes (Beresford 1998a).

1

Much of the research work that related to classroom practice explored pupils' perceptions of that practice. This focus reflected a growing interest, in the mid-1990s, in the pupil voice, and a belief that 'pupils' accounts of experience should be heard and should be taken seriously in debates about learning' (Rudduck *et al.* 1996a: 1). Not only was this voice 'astute and articulate' (Smees and Thomas 1998), it could also cast a unique and distinctive light upon the school environment. This interest arose partly from a growing concern within Western society for minors' rights, and partly as the result of a focus on consumers' rights which, in education, represented those of pupils as well as their parents (see, for example, Rudduck *et al.* 1996b; Beresford 1999a). Also important was the need, increasingly acknowledged in industrial societies, to prepare their school populations for lifelong learning, with learning becoming an increasingly essential part of their future working lives (Skilbeck 1994). Implicit in this growing interest was the view that learning took place more effectively where the needs of the learner were addressed. Part of the process of addressing these needs was canvassing the views of learners ('pupil' has been used as a generic term throughout the book to embrace those taught in primary and secondary schools).

In our IQEA project schools, teachers became increasingly interested in such a process. With the marginalisation of teacher control over curriculum content after the legislation of the late 1980s, the method of curriculum delivery became the main arena of teacher-pupil dialogue. Increasingly, the fieldwork I was asked by teachers to undertake in their schools involved questioning pupils about their learning.

Much of our published work focused upon developing 'capacity' – developing the capacity of schools and departments to pursue their own improvement agendas in a context of rapid educational change, developing the teaching capacity of teachers through the introduction, refinement and review of new teaching models and strategies in their classrooms. My own work with pupils, including observing them working in classrooms, led me to a belief that there was a complementary capacity, which the best teachers in our IQEA schools were developing – the learning capacity of their pupils. This book derives from this work, presenting ways in which teachers can develop such a learning capacity.

Pupil conditions for school improvement

The concept of conditions is employed in a variety of settings. Meteorologists study climatic conditions in an effort to forecast particular types of weather. Cricket commentators describe atmospheric and pitch conditions to forecast how a cricket pitch will 'play'. Health and safety inspectors are experts on the workplace conditions deemed necessary for safe working. Economists describe the conditions necessary for the economic 'take-off' of developing countries into large-scale industrial production. And school improvers write about the conditions necessary for school improvement to take place. Part of the agenda of school effectiveness research in the latter part of the last century was to demonstrate that changes in certain conditions could lead to school improvement (see, for example, Rutter *et al.* 1979; Mortimore *et al.* 1995).

School improvement has been defined as 'a systemic, sustained effort aimed at change in learning conditions, and other related internal conditions, in one or more schools, with the ultimate aim of accomplishing educational goals more effectively' (Van Velzen *et al.* 1985: 48). School improvement is thus clearly presented as a process rather than as an event. The conditions for school improvement refer to a set of prerequisites that enable an incremental growth in school effectiveness to take place. These constitute a set of conditions that need to be developed and maintained to make schools more effective. For school improvers, the development and maintenance of these conditions, and of a school's capacity to improve, are critical elements in their work with schools.

Within IQEA, we have devised sets of management (Ainscow *et al.* 2000) and classroom conditions (Hopkins *et al.* 1997) that we feel are necessary to develop within schools to enable them to build a capacity to effect and sustain school improvement. This book seeks to conceptualise a set of pupil conditions that are necessary to develop the learning capacity of pupils in such improving schools.

Developing pupils' learning capacity: the pupil conditions

Just as the early work in the IQEA project identified the need to address classroom-based as well as school-level conditions, subsequent work has suggested a need to further refine our approach to school improvement. In working more closely with pupils, it became increasingly apparent that

- pupils often had different views to teachers of what was happening in classrooms;
- pupils had their own views on how they learned best, and how they preferred their learning to be organised;
- teachers were interested in what were often insightful versions of pupil classroom activities, and welcomed advice on ways of canvassing these views;
- as well as developing their own teaching capacity, some teachers were actively employing certain techniques to develop their pupils' learning capacity.

This presented us with the notion that schools might need to work on three sets of interconnected and parallel conditions in order to enhance pupil learning – the school-level conditions relating to the management arrangements in the school, a set of classroom conditions that focused on developing teaching capacity and a further set focusing on the development of pupils' learning capacity. To avoid confusion, the set of classroom conditions that develop teaching capacity is referred to hereafter as the *teacher conditions*, those developing learning capacity as *pupil conditions*.

We were therefore able to refine our original framework for school improvement, shown in Figure 1.1.

The research questions for investigating the pupil conditions were similar to those researched for the original (teacher) conditions (Hopkins *et al.* 1997: 9):

- *conceptual issues*: What are the conditions that can help to develop the learning capacity of all pupils?
- *methodological issues*: How can pupils within a school present views on the extent to which these conditions are in place?
- *strategic issues*: How can teachers be helped to improve these conditions?

The required tasks identified during the investigation are set out in Table 1.1.

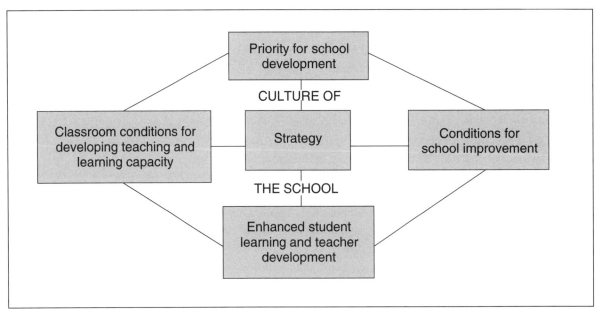

Figure 1.1 Refining the framework for school improvement (adapted from Hopkins *et al.* 1997: 8)

Table 1.1 Pupil conditions that help to develop the learning capacity of all pupils: research agenda and tasks (adapted from Hopkins *et al.* 1997: 9)

Research focus	Research questions	Tasks
Reconceptualising classroom (teacher) conditions	What are the pupil conditions that can help develop the learning capacity of all pupils?	Literature review and school-based observation and enquiry
Auditing pupil conditions	How can pupils within a school present views on the extent to which these conditions are in place?	Developing techniques for mapping pupil conditions
Developing pupil conditions	How can teachers be helped to improve these conditions?	Activities involving pupils to develop their learning capacity

The main body of research was undertaken as part of a PhD study between 1998 and 2001 (Beresford 2002), and included fieldwork in over 60 schools. The original teacher conditions needed to be reconceptualised for two reasons. First, some of the teacher activities described in the teacher conditions were invisible to pupils, for example those relating to planning and staff development undertaken by teachers, so pupils could not comment on them. Second, pupils had different views and different priorities related to their learning that were not reflected in the original teacher conditions. However, for the findings of the pupil conditions audit to be of use to teachers in planning activities to develop their pupils' learning capacity, the audit needed to address classroom behaviours with which teachers would be familiar. The resulting question-naires (one for secondary pupils and one for primary) appear in the Appendix. They are organised in the same format as the Management and Classroom (Teacher) Conditions Surveys that can be found in *Improving the Quality of Education for All* (Hopkins 2002: 120–5).

This handbook provides activities where teachers can interact with pupils to develop their learning capacity. It is intended as a companion to those previously published on developing school-level (Ainscow *et al.* 2000) and classroom (teacher) conditions (Hopkins *et al.* 1997).

Reconceptualising the classroom conditions: teacher and pupil conditions

The original classroom (teacher) conditions, and the reconceptualised (pupil) conditions are presented in Table 1.2. The descriptions of each teacher condi-tion are taken from the IQEA team's work on classroom conditions (Hopkins *et al.* 1997: 10).

In the process of reconceptualising the conditions it was necessary to iden-tify a set of classroom activities that:

- pupils would identify as being related to their learning;
- teachers would recognise as integral to the learning process;
- reflected the complementary processes of teaching and learning.

This was done by revisiting the literature of school improvement in order to identify the common ground trodden by teachers and pupils in responding to the requirements of living, working and learning at the turn of the century.

This period is characterised as one of unrelenting change: the expansion of international trade, the revolution in micro-electronics and communications, and the pace of technological change. These global developments have been likened by some writers (Giddens 1990; Barber 1996) to a juggernaut: 'a runaway engine of enormous power which, collectively as human beings, we can drive to some extent, but which also threatens to rush out of our control and which could render itself asunder' (Giddens 1990: 139). Mankind's main challenge is seen as coming to terms with and harnessing what is described as the global consequences of modernity, including protecting the environment and staving off war while countries compete for ever-diminishing amounts of natural resources. In such critical times, education for all becomes a necessity: 'No-one can completely opt out of the abstract systems involved in modern institutions' (*ibid.*: 84). Universal education is needed so that all can play their part in controlling the juggernaut, providing 'a guarantee of capacity to partici-pate' (Skilbeck 1994). Increasingly, governments in industrialised societies have viewed the development of this capacity in terms of providing 'a common experience for all pupils of whatever backgrounds or perceived abilities' (McLean 1990). In Japan, for example, the most recent revision of the Japanese Course of Study, their national curriculum, has tried 'to place more emphasis on basic and essential knowledge and skills required of every citizen of our country' (Yamagiwa 1994). In England the introduction of the National Curriculum in 1988 was in part to provide what some considered to be a better preparation for life at work and in society than the more humanities-based

Table 1.2 Teacher and pupil conditions

Teacher condition	Pupil condition
Reflection on teaching	**Self-assessment**
The capacity of the individual teacher to reflect on his or her own practice, and to put to the test of practice, specifications of teaching from other sources	*The ability of pupils to reflect upon and to improve the quality of their own work*
Planning for teaching	**Independent learning**
The access of teachers to a range of pertinent teaching materials and the ability to plan and differentiate those materials for a range of pupils	*The ability of pupils to access the skills and resources necessary to achieve learning autonomy*
Authentic relationships	**Affinity to teachers**
The quality, openness and congruence of relationships existing in the classroom	*The ability of pupils to maintain a relationship with teachers which enables them to seek and receive help and support when they require it*
Teaching repertoire	**Learning repertoire**
The range of teaching styles and models available for use by a teacher, dependent on pupil, context, curriculum and desired outcome	*The ability of pupils to exploit fully the range of teaching and learning strategies encountered in and out of the classroom*
Pedagogic partnerships	**Orientation to learning**
The ability of teachers to form professional relationships, within and outside the classroom, which focus on the study and improvement of practice	*The ability of pupils to be self-motivated, and to enjoy learning*
Boundaries and expectations	**Adjustment to school**
The pattern of expectations set by the teacher and school of pupil performance and behaviour within the classroom	*The ability of pupils to learn within a structured environment of rules and behaviour parameters*

curriculum of the 1970s and 1980s: 'The National Curriculum... tries to ensure that all pupils up to the age of 16 continue to study mathematics, sciences and technology which would otherwise be neglected in the preparation of aesthetes' (McLean 1990).

This development of the individual's 'capacity to participate' in a 'global economy of technological change' (Labour Party 1997: 3) has in part been in response to fundamental variations in workplace requirements brought about by the same technological change. Three main changes have been identified:

1. *The need for flexibility.* The need for business to be responsive to sudden changes in the global market, and for workers to be responsive to frequent changes in industrial technology, has spawned 'the appearance of a collection of industrial innovations, such as flexible specialised production, new uses of information-based technologies, flatter management structures, and the new emphasis upon teamwork' (Young 1993). Such a scenario provides a contrast to a fast-disappearing world where workers could rely upon single skills or unskilled work to provide them with a lifelong income. For example, in the motor industry simple skill applications have been replaced by a horizontal integration of skills, involving tasks at similar levels of competence' (Phillimore 1989). As unskilled jobs disappear, 'the requirement is for a work-force which is more flexible, more skilled and capable of continued learning' (Hughes 1994). This flexibility involves 'a preparedness to meet different requirements at different career stages' (Smith 1994).

2. *An increased emphasis on teamwork.* Because of the proliferation of knowledge and the pace of technological change, it is suggested that

   > no-one can become an expert, in the sense of the possession either of full expert knowledge or of the appropriate formal credentials, in more than a few small sectors of the immensely complicated knowledge systems which now exist.   (Giddens 1990: 144)

   This effectively means that even the simplest task may involve some degree of cooperation with others. In reviewing a curriculum for 2000, Ted Wragg (1997) suggested that 'as more jobs are created in service, leisure and recreation, the ability to get on with others becomes more valued'. BP, in its submission to the government prior to the introduction of the National Curriculum, called not only for a core of numeracy and literary skills but also for 'that range of personal transferable skills (e.g. communication, problem-solving, and team-work skills) which is so essential to effective participation in business life' (Haviland 1988: 32).

3. *A commitment to lifelong learning.* Because of the generation and increased availability of new knowledge related to the workplace, there is a need to encourage the development of 'well-rounded, technologically literate citizens who have some insight into the processes of scientific and technological development and the capacity and will to keep returning to the system to sharpen and broaden their skills and understanding' (Young 1993). In short, the information society 'requires the capacity not simply to learn new skills, but to keep on doing so' (Hughes 1994).

The reassessment of the skills and knowledge needed in the rapidly changing technologies of the late twentieth century has had implications for both teachers and learners in schools. Teachers themselves have been required to accommodate rapid change as pupils have been required to develop new learning habits to cope with the changes in their school and their future working lives. Teachers and pupils have been forced together as learners in a constantly changing learning culture.

This culture, in spite of its apparent state of perpetual motion, has some permanent features. These are as follows:

- *Learning has a central part in everyone's life.* A critical requirement in a society that depends for its well-being on rapid responses to technological change is that its young not only want to learn but *continue* to want to learn. Callaghan's Ruskin speech called for an education system that developed 'lively inquiring minds and the appetite for further knowledge that will last a lifetime' (Callaghan 1976). The government's aim of *Excellence for Everyone* called for an education system that would 'light a flame to provide a love of learning and a will to succeed for every child' (Labour Party 1995: 1). Such a requirement means that learning needs to be regarded as an enjoyable as well as a worthwhile activity. The government's recent initiative on teaching in the foundation subjects in Key Stage 3, with its 'focus on improving motivation and engagement' (DfEE 2001), recognises this. For the teacher, building appropriate attitudes to learning becomes 'a crucial part of teaching and learning' (Nisbet 1994). In effective classrooms, learning is talked about, aspects of learning (like homework) are explained and justified, and teachers and pupils get excited about learning. It is acknowledged as a struggle for some people, it is extolled, and the learning skills of peers are respected and used (Scottish CCC 1996; Doddington *et al.* 1999; Flutter *et al.* 1999). Teachers acknowledge that they are still learning, and collaborate with colleagues to trial and explore new ways of teaching (Hopkins *et al.* 1997). For the pupil, building such a self-image as a learner is equally crucial. The ability of pupils to respond to teacher motivation, to develop the self-motivation to want to continue learning when there is no teacher, and ultimately to enjoy learning, contributes collectively to a positive orientation to learning, a critical element of pupils' learning capacity.

- *The quality of relationships between teachers and learners is critical.* Clearly the emphasis upon teachers engaging and motivating pupils places a premium on good teacher-pupil relationships. The communication of knowledge at a time when knowledge is constantly proliferating is a process requiring a high degree of trust in those communicating, be they car mechanics, building labourers or teachers. Trust is required because those in receipt of the knowledge cannot possibly know more than a small part of the process being communicated.

  Where car mechanics or teachers fail to engage those with whom they are communicating, 'bad experiences at access points may lead either to a sort of resigned cynicism or...to disengagement from the system altogether' (Giddens 1990: 91). The need to engage is seen as the joint responsibility of communicator and receiver: 'Trust on a personal level becomes a project, to be 'worked at' by the parties involved, and demands the *opening out of the individual to the other* (*ibid.*: 121, emphasis in original). Crucially for the teacher, 'where it cannot be controlled by fixed normative codes, trust has to be won, and the means of doing this is demonstrable warmth and openness' (*ibid.*).

Teachers who show respect to their pupils, who are fair, who help them and show interest in them, who provide a safe environment for pupils to experiment with different behaviours and approaches to learning, and who pay attention to securing pupils' self-esteem are more likely to improve pupils' learning than those who ignore these aspects (Munn *et al.* 1990; Rudduck *et al.* 1996b; Morgan and Morris 1999).

For pupils, an affinity to teachers which enables them to maintain a relationship with staff, which allows them to seek and receive help and support when they require it, as well as to respond to the motivation already identified as an important factor in developing positive attitudes to lifelong learning, is an important pupil condition for improving learning in the classroom.

- *Learning is an orderly activity.* Most jobs, along with flexibility and creativity, require qualities of punctuality and cooperation, what the Confederation of British Industry described as 'the norms for behaviour in working situations' in its submission on the proposed education reforms of 1988 (Haviland 1988: 29). For schools, such working norms include attendance at school and adherence to codes of conduct in the classroom and outside. When pupils do not attend school, they may miss key elements of the learning necessary for their future working and social lives, for example the ability to work with others. Where they do not adhere to school behaviour norms, they may have the 'bad experiences at access points' referred to above by Giddens, which may in turn lead to disengagement and demotivation. Clearly this is less likely to happen where there is 'greater and more constructive pupil involvement in the planning and conduct of their education' (Hughes 1994) and where pupils have some say in the establishment of school norms: 'to teach about responsibility must imply a willingness to give responsibility' (Hughes and Skilbeck 1994).

  The maintenance of order in the classroom is widely recognised as a key element in effective lessons (Munn *et al.* 1990; Creemers 1994; Bleach 1997; Hopkins *et al.* 1997; Hopkins *et al.* 1998; Ofsted 1999: 39). Pupils learn best when they are clear about the parameters and rules system within the classroom. These elements contribute to what has been called elsewhere an 'authentic relationship' between teacher and pupils, that which 'seeks growth and empowerment, [and is] neither submissive nor subordinate, nor superior, but aligned with the pupils in following their endeavours and achieving the goals of the school' (Brandes and Ginnis 1990: 30).

- *Learning takes place in a variety of ways.* Within developing industrial countries, teachers need to use a range of teaching styles and strategies in order to make teaching more interesting to more pupils (Yamagiwa 1994), and to help pupils to learn how to learn and relearn (OECD 1994). Pupils need a battery of learning strategies to cope with the learning demands that might be made upon them in their future working lives and to solve work problems that require a range of skills and approaches (Young 1993). The development of learning autonomy, where learning can take place

9

independently of teaching, is fast becoming a key work skill: 'Learning in remote locations, with or without others, will become easier, so the ability to learn autonomously will be important' (Wragg 1997). The development of pupils' learning repertoire, where they are able to exploit fully the range of teaching and learning strategies encountered in and out of the classroom, is thus an important condition in enhancing pupil learning capacity.

Most current definitions of effective classroom teaching suggest that classroom teachers should employ a wide teaching repertoire (see, for example, Sammons *et al.* 1995; Harris 1995; Hopkins *et al.* 1997), that is, have at their fingertips a variety of ways of delivering the curriculum. This repertoire needs to cater for pupils of different ages and abilities in a variety of physical settings and groupings in order that an appropriate education can be delivered to all pupils (Creemers 1994), and so that the values and aspirations of teachers can 'infuse the ethos of their classrooms' (Hansen 1993).

Teachers are more likely to engender a respect for learning, and to embrace more of their pupils in the learning process, if they deploy a wide range of teaching strategies (Beresford 1999b). Teachers with a wide repertoire of teaching models are more able to adapt their teaching according to what they wish to teach (Blatchford and Kutnick 1996: Scottish CCC 1996; Joyce *et al.* 1997; Morgan and Morris 1999), to respond to the different learning styles of their pupils (Kolb 1984; Beresford 1999b) and to react flexibly and positively to negative pupil feedback during a lesson (Spaulding 1997).

- *Learning is a planned activity.* Learning on the job, either alone or in teams, has been identified as a key skill for the present and future workforce. For the pupil this translates into the ability to learn away from the teacher, for example at home or in groups. For teachers it means

  > Ensuring that pupils are actively involved in the learning process, are aware of where they need to improve, have the skills to make the necessary next steps and have the self-esteem and confidence to take on the challenge.
  > (DfEE 2001)

  It requires teachers to provide classroom opportunities to teach and develop independent learning skills – groupwork, paired work, independent research opportunities and problem-solving opportunities. Teachers need to plan both long-term programmes and short-term learning experiences for their pupils (Creemers 1994; Kyriacou 1998), taking into account the time and material resources available, the content they wish to teach and the characteristics of the pupils they are teaching, as well as their own teaching strengths (and weaknesses) (Brown and McIntyre 1993). It requires in pupils the ability to access the skills and resources necessary for them to achieve learning autonomy.

- *Teaching and learning is evaluated.* An important element of learning autonomy is the ability to reflect, self-assess and evaluate. The government's Key Skills Strategy (QCA 2000) recognises this importance. For example, it requires pupils at Level 1 who are seeking to improve their own learning and performance to 'give [their] opinion on what [they] have learned, how [they] have learned, what has gone well and what has gone less well'. At a higher level pupils are asked to 'assess [their] skill-development needs by identifying the gap between [their] current capabilities and the demands of the work in terms of communication, problem-solving and working with others' (*ibid.*). The ability to evaluate their own learning involves pupils in assessing the effectiveness and scope of their learning repertoire, their ability to learn independently, the quality of their relationships with their teachers and the extent of their adjustment to school expectations and norms. In short, the ability to reflect upon and to improve the quality of their own work is a 'linchpin' condition for pupils.

There is a long tradition of classroom-based action research providing data for the processes of reflection and evaluation of teaching. Teachers evaluate their teaching by assessing and monitoring their pupils' learning (Southworth 1998; Kyriacou 1998) and by inviting feedback from pupils (see King Harold School with the University of Cambridge Institute of Education 1995; Sharnbrook Upper School 1995). When such processes take place in a supportive school environment, then the collaborative structures are already in place to effect change and improvement, for example to replicate proven changes in teaching practice (Hayes and Ross 1989; Winston 1992).

Table 1.3 presents the two sets of teacher and pupil conditions, and the identified feature, or unifying principle, of the learning culture of which they are both a part. All three components emphasise the mutuality of teaching and learning while also showing their differences. They stress the need for reflection, for planning, for respect within the learning relationship and for diversity in the classroom, but through the different lenses of teacher and pupil. They provide a framework to make pupils more effective learners.

Table 1.3 Teacher and pupil conditions: the common ground

Teacher condition	Unifying principle	Pupil condition
Reflection on teaching	*Teaching and learning is evaluated*	Self-assessment
Planning for teaching	*Learning is a planned activity*	Independent learning
Authentic relationships	*The quality of relationships between teachers and learners is critical*	Affinity to teachers
Teaching repertoire	*Learning takes place in a variety of ways*	Learning repertoire
Pedagogic partnerships	*Learning has a central part in everyone's life*	Orientation to learning
Boundaries and expectations	*Learning is an orderly activity*	Adjustment to school

CHAPTER 2

Self-assessment

Those involved in the IQEA project, both external consultants and teachers, have identified enquiry and reflection as 'a most powerful classroom condition' (Hopkins *et al.* 1997: 92) because they perceive that

> teachers who are self-critical of their own practice as a matter of routine appear...to be those teachers who have the most extensively developed repertoires, and also seem to be the teachers who are most aware of the many things that are happening in the classroom at any one time.   (*ibid.*)

Within the project we have found that those schools in which teachers systematically collect and use classroom-based data, in part to evaluate the impact of their classroom practice, find it easier to sustain improvement efforts around established priorities, even in times of rapid change in education (see, for example, Hopkins *et al.* 1996; Beresford and Payne 1997; West and Beresford 1998).

In the same way that reflection and enquiry enable teachers to take control over, and personal responsibility for, their own teaching, we would argue that some degree of reflection enables pupils to exercise an element of control over, and responsibility for, their own learning. Our own research within IQEA suggests that some pupils do reflect on what they have done at school, and that homework is often the catalyst for such reflection. Pupils in schools where teachers have overtly used and discussed with them various teaching models and strategies show themselves able to articulate clearly about how they are taught, to evaluate the particular model or strategy and to discuss its appropriateness both for the subject under review and for other curriculum areas. The invitation to pupils to explore their own learning through explaining their thinking and problem-solving strategies is seen as an important teaching strategy in developing pupil self-assessment at both primary and secondary levels (Dann 1996; Scottish CCC 1996; Parker-Rees 1997; Norwich 1998; Assessment Reform Group 1999; Doddington *et al.* 1999; Flutter *et al.* 1999). Hand-in-hand with the understanding of how they are learning often comes an enjoyment of a particular teaching approach, and the motivation to do well. Where pupils are less clear about how they learn, they are more inclined to highlight personal shortcomings to account for their lack of success, which can impact upon both their motivation and their self-esteem as learners.

Teachers can undertake a series of strategies which can feed into this reflective process. They can explain and justify to pupils the purposes of the various teaching devices they employ, for example homework (Warrington and Younger 1996) and collaborative groupwork (Hubbard 1997). They can give clear guidance to pupils on what it means to work hard (Rudduck 1995; Kershner 1996; Maden and Rudduck 1997; Maden and Johnson 1998). Where pupils are involved in one-to-one discussions on the progress they are making and in class discussions, teachers can develop with them a language for thinking and talking about learning (Towler and Broadfoot 1992; Homerton-Schools Research Circle 1997). Target-setting has been proposed as one way of promoting a dialogue between teachers and pupils about pupil learning and performance (DfEE 1997).

An ongoing dialogue between teachers and pupils, using a shared language of teaching and learning, promotes a culture in which pupils are not afraid to ask for help (Black and Wiliam 1998a). Pupils we talked to in IQEA schools were prepared to ask teachers for help on how to improve their work where there was a culture of asking, for example in GCSE classes or where special needs pupils were present, where schools had set up a formal system of pupil mentoring or where pupils could approach teachers in private, and where requests for group help could be lodged anonymously.

As well as feedback and discussion about how they are learning, pupils clearly need feedback on *how well* they are learning. Self-assessment is an activity in which pupils, even those untutored in the necessary skills, routinely take part (Daniels and Welford 1990; Raynor 1995). Pupils we have interviewed within the project are dependent upon a range of sources in order to assess how well they are doing at school. Some of these sources are clearly flawed. Though pupils lay great emphasis, at least in the early years of secondary school, on the rewards system, many are clearly aware that their school is more generous in bestowing merits upon younger pupils for their motivational function than they are to pupils further up the school. Good marks appear to be given for different things in Years 7 to 9 than in Years 10 and 11 in a number of our schools. How a teacher relates to a particular pupil is also an important indicator for many, which suggests that some pupils may be unable to distinguish between teacher attitudes occasioned by their behaviour and those arising from their work performance. Those who see the number of punishments inflicted upon them as an indicator of how well they are doing are manifestly unable to make such a distinction.

The lengths of written comments at the end of pieces of work are often seen by pupils as being in inverse proportion to the quality of the piece. Pupils tell us that they would welcome occasional elaborative comment on what they have done *well*, in order for them to use such comments to plan future work. Teachers who share the criteria of what constitutes good work, along the lines of those provided for Year 9 pupils involved in coursework (Rudduck 1996b), provide pupils with an important element for self-assessment, particularly of work where the criteria are externally prescribed (Maden and Rudduck 1997; Assessment Reform Group 1999). While it is clear that some teachers facilitate pupil self-assessment to a degree by providing their pupils with quality criteria, details of the syllabus and helpful comments on how they can improve their work, it is hardly surprising that, given the confusing myriad of sources, many pupils in our IQEA schools, and elsewhere, are not very good at self-assessment (Daniels and Welford 1990; Raynor 1995).

Our own work suggests that pupils take seriously the business of reporting their own progress, and that pupils' parents are inquisitive about their progress in school, although the quality of feedback which they receive from their children is variable. It also suggests that this particular aspect of self-assessment may not be a high priority in schools. Where pupils are clear on the criteria for making judgements and assessments, they show themselves to be serious-minded in written self-assessments, though still inclined to inflate their own performances, and possibly those of their peers.

We would therefore conclude that pupils effectively assess their own progress when

- they reflect upon the work that they do (Activity 2.1);
- they get adequate feedback on how well they are doing at school (Activity 2.2);
- they make a meaningful contribution to the reporting of their own achievements (Activity 2.3);
- they are able to ask teachers how they can improve their own work (Activity 2.4).

Activity 2.1: pupil reflection on learning

Context

Getting pupils to think about what they have done in a lesson is a first step towards developing the skills of self-assessment which are necessary for autonomous learning to take place. Pupils are routinely provided with the aims and objectives at the start of lessons, and a review of the lesson at the end, but they are rarely asked for their views about whether the aims and objectives have been met. Such a simple strategy starts to involve pupils in their own education – talking about how they learn, assessing how effective particular teaching strategies have been in helping them learn and helping them focus upon the purpose of the lesson.

Briefing

Aims

- To provide pupils with an opportunity to reflect upon their learning.
- To provide teachers with feedback on how effective their teaching has been.

Process

The schedule is suitable for secondary and primary pupils, although some of the language might need to be explained or modified for very young pupils. It is presented in the form of a questionnaire, as some teachers might not feel ready, or feel that their pupils are not ready, to stage a discussion on effective learning at the end of a lesson. The schedule can, however, be used as a prompt for a discussion where teachers feel more confident.

The questionnaire should take less than ten minutes to complete. It does not need to be used for every lesson, but as pupils become more accustomed to filling it in, and where teachers find the feedback useful, it can be employed as a regular part of lesson review, giving away eventually to a meaningful discussion about teaching and learning between pupils and teacher at the end of every lesson.

LESSON REVIEW

I would like to know your views on the lesson that you have just had, so that I can adjust my teaching to help you learn more effectively. I would therefore be grateful if you could take a few minutes to answer the questions below as carefully as you can.

I don't need to know your name.

Date: _____   Class: _____

I am a   boy   girl   *(please circle the correct answer)*

Give a score to show how you feel about the following statements.

1 = strongly disagree   2 = disagree   3 = agree   4 = strongly agree

(please circle the score nearest to how you feel)

1.	I enjoyed the lesson	1	2	3	4
2.	I was very involved in the lesson	1	2	3	4
3.	I knew the aims and objectives of the lesson	1	2	3	4
4.	The lesson achieved its aims and objectives	1	2	3	4
5.	I understood what I had to do	1	2	3	4
6.	I could do all of the work I was asked to do	1	2	3	4
7.	I had plenty of time to complete the work	1	2	3	4
8.	I had all the books and equipment I needed in the lesson	1	2	3	4
9.	I listened well in the lesson	1	2	3	4
10.	I worked hard in the lesson	1	2	3	4

Complete these statements with your own views:

11. I thought the best part of the lesson was . . .

12. I learnt best in the lesson when . . .

13. The part of the lesson I liked least was . . .

14. What I would have changed in the lesson was . . .

Thank you for filling in this questionnaire.

          © John Beresford 2003 – Creating the Conditions to Involve Pupils in Their Learning

Activity 2.2: pupils knowing how well they are doing

Context

A key element of pupil self-assessment is pupils knowing how well and at what level they are working. Along with an awareness of how hard they are working, this knowledge can help pupils in the planning of their work, and can encourage them to seek help when they feel they need it. It provides pupils with the necessary self-knowledge to set meaningful work targets for themselves, in discussion with their teachers. Where pupils are clear about where they are and what they have to do to improve, more effective teaching and learning can take place.

Briefing

Aims

- To provide pupils with an opportunity to comment on methods of assessment in the school.
- To provide teachers with feedback on how pupils assess how well they are doing.

Process

The schedule is designed for use with groups of six to eight pupils. The questions are intended as prompts for pupils to elaborate on the various ways they are made aware of how well they are doing in school. The interviews are best conducted by a teacher who does not teach any of the pupils in the group, or by a learning assistant.

The schedule has been used with different year-groups within the same school, or with a group composed of representatives from different years. It has provided insights, for example, into how the reward system is viewed by different age-groups. The findings from the various interviews can be compared to provide a comprehensive review of the various forms of teacher assessment in the school and may lead, for example, to a policy review on the balance between summative and formative assessment routinely taking place in classrooms.

PROMPTS FOR ASSESSMENT DISCUSSION GROUPS

PUPILS

1. How do you know how well you're doing in your schoolwork?

2. Which ways are most common?

3. Which of these do you find most useful (examples of good practice) and why?

4. What do find least useful and why?

5. How does this knowledge help you to improve your work?
   (Does it?)

6. What differences are there across subject areas in the way that you get feedback? How would you describe a good piece of work in various subjects?

7. What motivates you/makes you work harder? Is it praise, the ethos of the school, our commendation system, reports home, etc.?

8. Have you any suggestions for ways in which the present system could be improved?

 © John Beresford 2003 – Creating the Conditions to Involve Pupils in Their Learning

Context

When pupils are involved in reflecting on what and how they learn at school, and are aware of how well they are doing and what they have to do to improve, pupil involvement in communications about attainment between the school and their homes becomes more meaningful. We have heard many complaints from pupils in schools where they are not involved in such reflection that their contributions to reports home are often tokenistic, and consist of what they think their teachers and parents want to hear. Involving pupils in self-reporting is another critical contribution to the development of self-assessment because it gives concrete form to the value that the school attributes to its pupils' views on teaching and learning, and it highlights the importance the school places on pupils' involvement in their own learning.

Briefing

Aims

- To enable pupils (and parents) to have some input into the format of reports from school to home.
- To provide a strategy for schools to review the formats of these reports.

Process

This activity is organised in five stages and suggests one approach to a review of the format of reports on pupil attainment that schools periodically send to parents. Step 1 involves teachers identifying what they see as the main purposes of such reports, and assessing the extent to which the school's current format serves those purposes. Step 2, in the event of the format in use being deemed inadequate, involves the setting up of a small working party, consisting perhaps of two teachers, two parents and two pupils, to discuss various ways of obtaining similar information from the pupil and parent bodies. In Step 3, the chosen methods of data collection are organised. Step 4 then involves the collation of the data by the working party, and Step 5 the presentation of the findings to the various interested parties. If a new format is to be piloted, the working party might also want to organise an interim evaluation.

Step 1   Depending on the number of your teaching staff, discuss in groups or as a whole staff the purposes of reports home to parents. Record responses so that they can be passed on to the working party.

Purposes of reports home:

Communication of pupils' attainments to parents

Communication of pupils' effort levels to parents

Information on how pupils learn most effectively

. . . . .

Now discuss whether the format of the reports currently in use in the school meets these requirements. You will need to come to a decision as a whole staff. If it is generally felt that the current format is adequate, it will not be necessary to proceed further.

Step 2   If the format is deemed to be inadequate, a working party can be set up to explore the views of pupils and parents on alternative formats. The working party should include representatives of teachers, pupils and parents. There might already be formal pupil and parent organisations in existence, like school councils and PTAs, which can be approached to nominate members.

© John Beresford 2003 – Creating the Conditions to Involve Pupils in Their Learning

Step 3   The working party meets and examines ways of collecting data, similar to that
                collected in Step 1, from pupils and parents.

Ways of collecting data:

```
Use of questionnaires

By interview

Delegation of tasks to PTA and school council

. . . . .
```

Step 4   After choosing ways of collecting data, the working party helps in the organ-
                isation of the collection. It then collates the data.

Step 5   The working party then presents its findings. It might want to consider the
                following questions, as part of its deliberations:

> - In what form do we present the findings? Do we provide a suggested
>   format for the reports?
> - How do we disseminate the findings? Can we use established meet-
>   ings like staff meetings, PTA meetings and tutorial periods? Do we
>   make a separate presentation to senior management?
> - Do we need to organise methods of feedback on its appropriateness
>   if a new format is to be piloted?

Activity 2.4: asking teachers for help

Context

Building a classroom culture where pupils are not inhibited about asking questions related to their work is an important element of making pupils autonomous learners. Pupils we have asked about seeking help in the classroom often hold back from asking such questions because they wish to avoid being called 'boffs' by their peers or looking stupid in front of their classmates. They are also keen to avoid risking the retribution of teachers and being accused of not listening. They often resort to consulting their neighbours and friends in the class, which sometimes lands them in trouble for talking, or alternatively they wait until the evening when they can complete tasks with the help of parents or older siblings. The teacher is the main learning resource in any classroom, and a culture which denies any pupils access to that resource needs to be changed.

Briefing

Aims

- To challenge any classroom culture that inhibits pupils asking teachers for help with work.
- To determine, in consultation with pupils, various ways in which teacher help can be accessed in the classroom.

Process

This activity consists of two steps. Step 1 involves the initiation of a discussion with pupils by the class teacher on the importance of seeking help in the classroom. Because asking for help in understanding tasks is so fundamental in the development of pupils as learners, this discussion should ideally take place early in the school year, certainly during the first few lessons with a new class. The teacher should seek to challenge each of the inhibiting factors identified by pupils. Step 2, if deemed necessary, involves introducing various ways in which pupils can 'signal' to the teacher that they need help. They include 'traffic-lighting', a technique described in *Working Inside the Black Box* (Black *et al.* 2002).

Step 1   Discuss with your class the importance in their development as learners of being able to access a variety of learning resources – books, CD-ROMs, the Internet, as well as teachers themselves. With the class, brainstorm factors that have inhibited them from asking their teachers for help in the past. Next, address each of these inhibiting factors in turn, trying to reach some consensus with the class that none provide sufficient grounds for holding back the learning process.

Step 2   This second stage should only be necessary where you have become aware, after the discussion, of some pupils who are still not seeking your help, even when they do not fully understand a task. Your own marking might give you some indication of this, and you might find the schedule in Activity 2.1 useful in gauging class levels of understanding.

Discuss with the class ways that they can access help from you. Some of the following may be useful.

Traffic-lighting   Pupils are each given three coloured discs – one green, one orange and one red. When they are confident about how to do a task, they leave a green disc exposed on their desks. When they are less sure, they expose an orange disc, and when they have little understanding of a task, they expose the red disc. Teachers can then see at a glance where their help is needed, without pupils having to put up their hands. Pupils can also use the appropriate colour, at the end of pieces of written work, to indicate whether they fully, partly or inadequately understood the work they have just completed. Paul also suggests that, in revision periods, pupils can respond in a similar way about their understanding of key words and concepts identified by the teacher.

White-boarding   This is a technique now commonly used in many primary and secondary classrooms, whereby every pupil is required to write on his or her own whiteboard an answer to a teacher's question. This has the advantages of giving all pupils time to answer the question, and of requiring an answer from all pupils that only the teacher can see, since the whiteboards are pointed in the teacher's direction. Pupils do not face potential public humiliation by having to respond verbally: teachers can make a mental note of those pupils who have given a wrong answer, and who may need further support, and all answers disappear with the wipe of a cloth.

Peer coaching   This strategy would allow pupils to discuss with their immediate neighbour the requirements of a particular task, and would hopefully facilitate understanding without resort to the teacher. Such a strategy might require careful seating arrangements whereby more articulate or able pupils are seated next to those who are less so.

Pupils may themselves come up with some ingenious 'signalling' strategies of their own device, or ones that their previous teachers have employed.

CHAPTER 3

Independent learning

The ability of pupils to learn independently is an important element in their development as learners. Where we have identified the planning of teaching as a key classroom condition for improving teaching and learning in schools, we would argue that the ability of pupils to organise their own learning is a complementary skill that needs to be addressed by teachers.

In a world where the classroom teacher is now only one of a burgeoning number of knowledge sources, pupils need to develop a battery of independent learning and problem-solving skills and techniques in order to process and learn from the wide information base now available. They need to develop and refine their own learning strategies so that they can benefit fully from the variety of learning situations that they meet as pupils, and in later life as citizens and workers.

Those commentators reviewing the curricular requirements of a society in the midst of a micro-electronic revolution in communications and information technology suggest that the working population will need to learn and relearn new skills as a matter of routine during their working lives (Wragg 1997). The ability to learn independently is 'one of the most oft-cited goals of schooling' (Levin 1995), one which schools need to address by giving pupils 'tasks or projects which require some sustained effort over time, and then give them the ability and the scope to organise themselves to pursue these projects' (*ibid.*). It is also argued that the learning autonomy provided through independent learning gives concrete recognition to the individuality of learners (Kaminski 1999), and symbolises, on the part of teachers, 'respect for the child's ability to grapple with intellectual problems' (Gracie 1981). In moving their pupils towards learning autonomy, teachers need to redefine their classroom role. They need to become 'relaxed consultants' rather than 'charismatic animators' (Bowyer 1981), in other words the emphasis in teachers' classroom activity needs to shift from whole-class presentation to facilitating individual learning (Gibbs 1989). One of our IQEA secondary schools on the edge of Derby coaches its Year 7 cohort on independent learning strategies during their first week of school. Pupils are taught and given practice sessions in activities like cooperative groupwork, brainstorming and circle discussions, where the teacher chairs (but does not otherwise participate in) a class discussion. The staff, knowing that pupils have some expertise in a range of independent learning situations, include appropriate activities within their lesson plans to use and develop this expertise.

There is considerable evidence that pupils value this learning autonomy. They are enthusiastic about practical work (Osborne and Collins 1999), lab-work (Gonzalez and Gilbert 1980) and groupwork (Hazelwood *et al.* 1988; MORI/Campaign For Learning 1998). Undertaking projects in secondary schools gives meaning to work and a sense of ownership of related learning for participating pupils (Wallace 1996a; Rudduck 1996a). IQEA schools describe a range of classroom-based independent learning activities – researching from books, discussions, using ICT – and pupils are given varying degrees of opportunity to take part in them. Pupils in these schools generally regard themselves as able to access the resources they need to take advantage of such learning activities. Some pupils described opportunities outside the classroom, such as visits to the school library and other areas on the school site. We have found that pupils generally prefer these learning opportunities to those that are more teacher-centred. Inevitably, because of the demands of a prescribed curriculum and public examinations, much of the research pupils do has a strong element of teacher direction, with teachers setting the research questions and either distributing resources or directing pupils to the various sources of information inside and outside the classroom. This has been described as 'semi-independent learning' (Kaminski 1999).

One of the roles of teachers in developing learning autonomy is to build upon their pupils' 'craft knowledge' (Hubbard 1997), that which helps pupils to 'make sense of their learning situation and actively construct and develop their own learning strategies' (*ibid.*). The opportunity to apply existing knowledge to new situations through problem-solving is thus an important element in the development of pupils' ability to learn independently. Pupils suggest that only maths teachers consistently provide such opportunities, although instances are cited in science, personal and social education and drama. It may be that teachers of subjects other than maths feel that their pupils have an insufficient knowledge base to attempt problem solving effectively. Our experience is that the often protracted nature of problem-solving activities militates against teachers, under pressure to complete schemes of work, allocating time to them.

Homework requiring research appears to be the most common opportunity offered to pupils to learn independently, or semi-independently, of teachers. Pupils use school libraries, local libraries and home-based resources, including CD-ROMs, PC encyclopaedias, the Internet, books and parents to undertake research. In some schools pupils are coached in library skills, note-taking techniques and in background reading.

Another of the critical skills needed to develop pupils' learning autonomy is the ability to work effectively in groups. The skill is important because 'interaction among children around appropriate tasks increases their mastery of critical concepts' (Slavin 1993). Our own research suggests that the incidence of groupwork in schools is greater than the incidence of problem solving, and it is a strategy that is apparently used across the curriculum. It is a learning activity which pupils enjoy: they like the comfortable ambience of working in a group, the variety of ideas that circulate in group discussion, the speed of producing work that effective groupwork can achieve, and the quality of that work. Groupwork appears to be most effective where pupils are proficient in groupwork techniques, through custom and practice or by teachers coaching pupils in such techniques (Joyce *et al.* 1997). Teachers and support staff in a Year 6 class in a Merthyr primary school modelled a cooperative groupwork activity in front of the class, inviting pupils to comment upon how effectively they felt the activity was undertaken. The subsequent discussion enabled the staff to derive from the pupils some principles of effective groupwork, on which future work could be based.

Groupwork appears to be ineffective when pupils do not interact, or when they argue with each other or 'mess around'. This may be through lack of practice: pupils may have done an insufficient amount of groupwork to become conversant with ways of working effectively in groups. In such a situation, the opportunity to move away from a predominantly teacher-centric mode of learning may provide too great a temptation to socialise, hence the identification of groupwork, by both teachers and pupils in some of our schools, with 'bad' behaviour.

Independent learning therefore seems to take place when pupils

- feel they have ready access to the resources they need in lessons (Activity 3.1);
- are given opportunities to apply the knowledge they have acquired in problem-solving situations (Activity 3.2);
- take part on a regular basis in groupwork (Activity 3.3);
- undertake independent research activities (Activity 3.4).

Activity 3.1: making resources accessible to pupils

Context

Ensuring access to the books and equipment necessary for taking a full part in lessons is an important element in developing pupils' independent learning skills. Pupils who can access resources when they need them are able to plan the pace of their own work efforts, and in tasks requiring research they are also able to plan the content. Where resources are accessible, pupils are less dependent upon teachers for direction, and there is less disruption to the flow of the lesson. Readily available resources in the classroom reflect the trust teachers place in their pupils not only to look after the resources, but also to exercise some control over their own learning.

Briefing

Aims

- To identify through observation where 'bottle-necks' occur in classrooms.
- To ensure that pupils can access the books and equipment necessary for task completion in lessons.

Process

The following three-part activity will be particularly appropriate to primary school teachers and to those secondary teachers who do most of their teaching in one main teaching base. Step 1 involves briefing a colleague, perhaps a classroom assistant, to note down in a particular lesson (or series of lessons) the resources that pupils are required or choose to use, and also to note down where those resources are located in the classroom. In Step 2, the colleague 'maps' a lesson in this way, making notes about where and when pupil congestion occurs. Step 3 gives the teacher an opportunity, if necessary, to reorganise the teaching base in such a way that pupil access to resources is better facilitated.

Step 1   Brief a colleague, perhaps another teacher or a classroom assistant, to note down in a lesson (or series of lessons) the resources that pupils access, and where those resources are located in the classroom. You might want to provide them with a basic map of your classroom, and also a pro forma for their observations, similar to the one below.

Date:		Lesson:
Time	What pupils are accessing	Notes

Step 2   Your colleague 'maps' the lesson, making notes of any difficulties of access on the map and/or on the observation sheet.

Step 3   With the data collected, you might choose to reorganise the layout of your classroom to make resources more accessible. It might also be beneficial, in the light of the resources required by pupils, to make more or different kinds of resources available. Would the colleague who has been observing be willing to assess in the near future the impact of any changes you make?

      © John Beresford 2003 – Creating the Conditions to Involve Pupils in Their Learning

Activity 3.2: providing pupils with problem-solving activities

Context

The ability to apply knowledge and skills to solving problems is an important life skill. The ability to problem-solve gives overt justification to much of the curriculum delivered in schools, and it allows pupils to work independently on tasks that, if designed with care, can consolidate and even heighten pupils' appreciation and understanding of what they have learned. Problem-solving activities provide opportunities for teachers to assess how effectively their pupils have absorbed the knowledge and mastered the skills necessary to complete the tasks. While such tasks seem to be set routinely in maths and technology, they are less common in other subjects. In history, for example, pupils who have been taught about identifying historical bias and who have some knowledge of the First World War might be asked to comment on three or four different contemporary versions of its causes. In modern foreign languages, pupils with dictionary skills and a limited technical vocabulary could be asked to translate an unseen piece that contains a number of words and grammatical structures that they do not know.

Briefing

Aims

- To provide pupils with problem-solving activities across a range of subjects.
- To provide a simple format that teachers can use to plan problem-solving activities.

Process

This activity is aimed at teachers, although it has been suggested that pupils with a detailed knowledge of performance criteria, for example those who are about to sit GCSE examinations, benefit from undertaking problem-solving activities that they themselves have devised (Black *et al.* 2002: 13). The activity is best done with a colleague, in a secondary school with a colleague in the same subject department. After trying out the activity with different groups of pupils, and comparing experiences, teachers can add it to a central pool of such activities for future use.

Below is a format that you might find useful for planning a problem-solving activity. Discuss and refine the activity with a colleague. One or both of you can try it with pupils and, depending on its effectiveness, it can be 'stored' and used again in future years. Assessing its effectiveness should involve feedback from the pupils about the activity.

PROBLEM-SOLVING ACTIVITY

SUBJECT: YEAR-GROUP UNDERTAKING ACTIVITY:

Activity devised by: Date:

Assumed skills of pupils (NC Level ___)

Assumed knowledge of pupils

Outline of task to be done   *Resources required*

Anticipated process

N.B. Some pupils might provide solutions to the problem that do not necessarily follow the process that you have anticipated.

        © John Beresford 2003 – Creating the Conditions to Involve Pupils in Their Learning

Activity 3.3: making groupwork effective

Context

Being able to work effectively in teams is another important life-skill. Collaborative groupwork in the classroom is also an extremely effective learning strategy because it enables pupils to process knowledge collectively, and to rehearse and develop their knowledge and understanding in a less formal and less public arena than in front of the whole class. However, for collaborative groupwork to be effective, pupils need to be in possession of specific social skills. Where these social skills are lacking in appreciable numbers of pupils in a class, groupwork often deteriorates into a noisy and dysfunctional activity. These social skills therefore need to be made explicit, and teachers might need to coach their pupils in some of the specific skills, for example how to listen well and how to show respect for the opinions of others.

Briefing

Aims

- To involve pupils in the identification of the key skills necessary for effective groupwork to take place.
- To provide a framework whereby pupils can assess both their own groupwork skills and those of pupils with whom they work regularly.
- To establish a code of good practice for collaborative groupwork activities.

Process

The following activity has been used successfully with both primary and secondary classes and incorporates five steps. Step 1 involves brainstorming with pupils the features of effective groupwork, expressed in terms of what individual pupils do. A set of possible responses has been provided. Step 2 requires the teacher to present the responses in the form of a code of good practice. In Step 3, pupils have the opportunity to assess both their own groupwork skills and those of their classmates, using the responses generated in Step 1 and an assessment score-sheet. A possible format for the assessment sheet is given. Instructions for the periodic adminstration of the assessment instrument are provided in Step 4. Step 5 involves the analysis of the various pupil assessments, and the teacher's use of them to highlight the particular groupwork skills that need further development in the class.

Step 1

Set your class a groupwork activity and, after pupils have fed back on what they have done, start to discuss the process of groupwork with them. Ask prompting questions like 'Which groups feel they worked well?' and 'What did you do in the groups that made them work well?'. Start putting pupils' responses into a list, and invite the class to suggest other features of good groupwork practice. Your list may look something like the one below.

An effective groupworker:

1   Gets down to work quickly

2   Does not waste time

3   Takes their turn fairly

4   Does their fair share of work

5   Does not say they know everything

6   Helps us with what they know about the work

7   Asks us questions to help them understand what needs to be done

8   Knows where to find information to help us to do the work

9   Is open about how they feel and what they think

10   Is easy to understand

11   Gives others in the group a chance to talk

12   Listens well to others

13   Doesn't always agree with the rest of us

14   Is very thoughtful about what they say

15   Uses other people's ideas as well as their own

16   Often comes up with unusual but good ideas

17   Doesn't mind when others disagree with them

18   Doesn't blame others when mistakes are made

19   Carries on working hard when work is difficult

20   Always believes that work can be done

 © John Beresford 2003 – Creating the Conditions to Involve Pupils in Their Learning

Step 2   Having achieved a consensus with your class on what constitutes good practice in collaborative groupwork, produce a code of conduct that can be posted in the classroom as an *aide-mémoire* for pupils. One based on the 20 points listed above might resemble the following.

In this class, when we work in groups we

- Get on with the work

- Take turns in speaking

- Help each other

- Listen to each other

- Make helpful comments

- Think hard

- Keep going, even when things are difficult

Step 3   Once your pupils have had a number of opportunities to undertake collaborative groupwork, and are familiar with the components of effective groupwork, you will want to check periodically how well the class is functioning in groups. It is often difficult and obtrusive to observe and assess such activity yourself, but it is comparatively easy to devise an instrument whereby pupils can assess both themselves and those with whom they work. A format, based on the 20 features of good practice identified in Step 1, is reproduced below, and instructions on how to administer the instrument and analyse the results are provided in Step 4.

Groupwork skills observed by you and your friends

ME									
1	1	1	1	1	1	1	1	1	1
2	2	2	2	2	2	2	2	2	2
3	3	3	3	3	3	3	3	3	3
4	4	4	4	4	4	4	4	4	4
5	5	5	5	5	5	5	5	5	5
6	6	6	6	6	6	6	6	6	6
7	7	7	7	7	7	7	7	7	7
8	8	8	8	8	8	8	8	8	8
9	9	9	9	9	9	9	9	9	9
10	10	10	10	10	10	10	10	10	10
11	11	11	11	11	11	11	11	11	11
12	12	12	12	12	12	12	12	12	12
13	13	13	13	13	13	13	13	13	13
14	14	14	14	14	14	14	14	14	14
15	15	15	15	15	15	15	15	15	15
16	16	16	16	16	16	16	16	16	16
17	17	17	17	17	17	17	17	17	17
18	18	18	18	18	18	18	18	18	18
19	19	19	19	19	19	19	19	19	19
20	20	20	20	20	20	20	20	20	20

MY INITIALS ARE_____

 © John Beresford 2003 – Creating the Conditions to Involve Pupils in Their Learning

Step 4

Below are instructions on how to administer the assessment instrument introduced in Step 3, and how to analyse the results. If you have been able to persuade other colleagues to use the instrument, the instructions need to be very explicit.

GROUPWORK SKILLS: GUIDANCE FOR TEACHERS

1. Each student should be given his or her own copy of the groupwork skills (it's a useful *aide-mémoire*).
2. Each student should be given a blank score-sheet (the one with MY INITIALS ARE at the bottom).
3. Students should enter their own initials in the space provided. (In the event of two students having the same initials, negotiate an alternative. Remember to tell the rest of the class of the alternative.)
4. Ask the students to circle on the score-sheet in the 'ME' column which of the 20 skills they think they personally show in groupwork.
5. Then ask them to put the initials of students they regularly work with in groups in the spaces provided at the tops of the columns, one set of initials in each (don't forget to use any agreed alternatives to avoid confusion).
6. Ask the students to circle on their score-sheets each of the skills which the students they have entered in each column show during groupwork.
7. Take in the score-sheets, and collate the results for each student.

Example (Student AB)
Find AB's own sheet including her own self-assessment. Find other sheets where AB has been assessed by other students. Tally her score for each number, and work out her 'score' as a percentage of all her group members. If two people have circled number 8 for AB, and eight students have assessed her, then her score for 8 is 25(%). On a blank matrix, record AB's percentage scores for each skill. Shade in those numbers circled by AB. If she feels she has a skill but only a small percentage of her group agrees with her, she has a clear signal that she needs to work on that skill. A copy of a collated sheet can be seen in Step 5.

Step 5

You now need to analyse the data for your class. A sample table of results is given on p. 37 showing what an analysis of results may look like.

Example (Student KL)
The numbers down the left-hand side of the table refer to the 20 identified qualities of good groupwork. The numbers along the top are the numbers of pupils in the class who offered assessments of the pupil below. Hence five pupils have assessed 'KL'. The shaded squares indicate the qualities identified by pupils in their own self-assessments. The numbers inside the boxes refer to the percentage of their work colleagues who also identify the quality

in the particular individual. So, for example, 'KL' feels that he/she does not demonstrate Quality 9, but 80% of his/her workmates disagree. 'KL' feels that he/she was good at Qualities 3–5, 7, 8, 10–16 and 18–20, and not so good at 1, 2, 6, 9 and 17. The percentage scores show that his/her friends agree with 'KL' about 17, and are not as enthusiastic about his/her performance in 19 as 'KL' is. Collectively, the class does not self-assess itself highly on 1, 2, 6, 10 and 14. Regarding the groups themselves (indicated by the dark vertical lines), 'JP, AE, JW and AW' score each other poorly for 2, and 'SW, KD, CR and CJ' score each other low on 9. The teacher might want to address both the class and group issues at some future time.

© John Beresford 2003 – Creating the Conditions to Involve Pupils in Their Learning

	3	3	3	3	4	4	4	4	4	3	3	3	3	3	3	3	3	5	5	5	5	5	5
	AW	JW	AE	JP	DR	AR	JS	OW	SB	CJ	LG	LJ	AD	CJ	CR	KD	SW	JM	RG	JC	DR	DW	KL
1	0	33	100	33	100	75	100	50	50	67	67	33	100	67	33	33	33	100	60	100	80	0	60
2	0	0	33	33	100	50	75	25	50	67	67	0	100	67	33	33	33	80	80	80	80	40	60
3	33	67	100	100	100	100	100	50	50	67	67	33	67	100	100	100	100	80	80	100	60	60	80
4	67	100	100	100	100	100	100	25	50	67	67	33	67	67	100	100	*100	80	80	100	60	60	80
5	0	67	100	33	75	50	75	25	0	67	67	67	0	100	100	100	100	40	80	80	80	20	60
6	0	33	33	67	50	100	100	50	50	67	67	67	100	67	33	67	100	60	80	80	60	60	60
7	33	67	33	67	100	100	100	100	50	67	67	33	67	67	33	67	33	80	80	100	80	40	80
8	100	67	67	67	50	75	100	75	50	67	67	0	100	67	100	100	100	60	60	100	100	80	60
9	67	67	33	100	100	50	100	75	75	33	67	67	67	0	33	0	0	60	80	80	80	20	80
10	33	0	67	33	75	75	75	100	50	67	67	0	33	100	100	67	100	80	60	100	80	40	60
11	67	67	100	100	75	50	100	50	25	67	67	0	67	100	100	100	100	80	60	40	80	60	60
12	33	33	100	67	100	100	100	100	50	67	67	33	67	67	67	67	67	80	60	100	100	40	80
13	67	100	100	100	75	50	100	75	50	67	67	33	67	67	100	67	67	20	60	100	40	60	60
14	33	0	33	33	75	100	100	100	25	67	67	0	67	67	100	100	100	80	60	80	100	40	80
15	33	67	100	100	75	100	100	100	100	67	67	33	100	100	100	67	100	100	80	80	80	60	80
16	67	33	100	33	75	75	75	75	25	67	67	0	67	100	100	67	33	60	60	100	100	60	20
17	67	67	100	67	50	50	75	100	75	67	33	33	33	67	100	100	0	80	40	100	60	20	60
18	33	67	100	100	50	75	50	50	25	67	67	33	33	100	33	67	100	80	20	80	80	80	40
19	33	33	67	67	75	50	75	25	25	67	33	0	67	67	100	33	0	100	80	100	80	20	80
20	100	67	67	100	75	100	75	50	50	67	67	67	100	100	100	100	100	60	60	100	80	60	80

TABLE OF RESULTS

Activity 3.4: facilitating independent research

Context

Being able to access a variety of sources of information, and to use the information derived to consolidate and build upon personal levels of knowledge and understanding, are important skills for both school-based and lifelong learning. Directing pupils to key information sources, and providing them with the skills to process the information they retrieve, are important functions of teachers. We are surprised, when working with schools, at how little attention is given by teachers to coaching the skills involved in such processes as note-taking, and how few teachers are aware of the resources available to pupils at or near their homes. Schools, for example, are often surprised at the high proportion of their pupils who have access to the Internet at home.

Briefing

Aims

- To suggest a format whereby teachers can audit the resources available to pupils for independent research activities, and pupils' skills in using them.
- To enable teachers to highlight the information-processing skills that need addressing in their pupils.
- To enable teachers to set appropriate independent research activities for their pupils.

Process

The suggested format for the audit of resources and skills is based upon a number of examples that have been used successfully in IQEA schools. As with all of the suggestions in these activities, teachers are free to tailor formats to their own particular needs. This activity involves three steps. Step 1 entails drawing up and administering the audit, Step 2 involves the analysis of the results and Step 3 the planning of activities to develop the skills that pupils have identified as being problematic. The questions in the format can be used as prompts for teachers who want to undertake a less formal audit in a class-work session.

© John Beresford 2003 – Creating the Conditions to Involve Pupils in Their Learning

Step 1   Devise a questionnaire or set of questions that you wish to ask your pupils about what resources are available to them at or near their homes, and what particular skills they feel they need help with in accessing and processing the information. You might want to keep a record of individual responses, in which case it is advisable to use a questionnaire. Alternatively you might want a broader picture, in which case the questions can be asked to the whole class verbally, in a classwork session. The format below may be a useful starting point.

SKILLS AND RESOURCES AUDIT

Teachers in the school want to help you to become better independent learners. Being able to research information is an important independent learning skill, and we want to be able to equip you with the necessary skills to do research, as well as give you opportunities to research at home. To do this we need some information about you. Please answer honestly, because this is for your benefit as much as ours.

My name is _____ I am in class _____

1. Please tick which of these apply to you:

I have access to the Internet at home, or at a friend's or relative's house	
I have CD-ROMs, like Encarta, at home	
I have a recent set of encyclopaedias at home	
I have access to dictionaries at home	
I have access to a range of reference books at home	
My nearest public library is within walking distance of home	

Other things at home that help me with my learning are (please state):

2. Please tick which of these apply to you:

I would like help to find suitable Internet websites to help my learning	
I would like help with how to read to extract information	
I would like help with how to use reference books	
I would like help with how to take notes	
I would like help with using a library catalogue	

Other research skills that I would like help with are (please state):

Thank you for filling in this questionnaire.

Step 2	You now need to analyse the results of your survey, whether you have used the questionnaire or a head-count in a class session.

Step 3	You are now in a position to identify the skills that large numbers of your pupils feel less confident about, and to organise activities that provide you with opportunities to coach those skills.

© John Beresford 2003 – Creating the Conditions to Involve Pupils in Their Learning

CHAPTER 4

Affinity to teachers

The centrality of teacher-pupil interactions in effective learning is well established. The quality of teachers' relationships with their pupils has been identified as one of the most important of 224 variables identified in one study as contributing to effective teaching (Wang *et al.* 1993). The creation of a classroom climate conducive to learning is identified as a key teaching skill (Scottish CCC 1996; Kyriacou 1998). The closeness of pupil-teacher relationships appears to impact upon the effectiveness of teacher assessment (Black and Wiliam 1998b), upon good order in the classroom (Haroun and O'Hanlon 1997; West and Beresford 1998; Morgan and Morris 1999), upon the attendance rates of former truants (Testerman 1996) and even upon the development of literacy skills (Campbell 1986). The importance of teachers as behaviour models for pupils has contributed to the disquiet over the decreasing number of males attracted to the teaching profession (Lahelma *et al.* 1999). There is some suggestion that the interpersonal skills of head teachers are important elements in defining pupil attitudes to school (Day *et al.* 2000). Pupils in Higher Education have reported lasting and often fond memories of their primary teachers' personalities and attitudes (Hayes 1993).

Our own research within IQEA has highlighted the importance of these 'authentic relationships' as a major determinant of pupil progress, where teachers establish the classroom

> as a safe and secure learning environment in which pupils can expect acceptance, respect and even warmth from their teachers, without having to earn these – they are intrinsic rights which are extended to pupils because they are there.
> (Hopkins *et al.* 1997: 14)

Like many others in the school improvement field, we have derived this view in part by talking directly to pupils about their teachers. We have found that pupils respond best to teachers who show an active interest in them as people as well as learners (see Marzano *et al.* 1992; Chaplain 1996b). Pupils in our IQEA schools have confirmed that teacher friendliness is 'immensely important' to them (Wallace 1996b), and that they dislike teachers who are strict. Secondary pupils in particular show strong feelings for justice, equity and respect, and confirm that 'when teachers trust and respect young people as learners and thinkers and as people, and let them see this, they are much more likely to receive trust and respect in return' (Scottish CCC 1996: 16).

Pupils dislike stereotyping, or 'image-fixing' (Day 1996) of pupils by teachers and the administration of group punishments as a result of the behaviour of a few. Pupils also value helpful teachers, those who are approachable and can explain well (Wallace 1996b; Black and Wiliam 1998a). We have found that the withholding of teacher help, for whatever reason, is often taken as a personal slight by pupils who are experiencing work difficulties.

Feelings about their teachers dominate and, to a considerable extent, mould pupils' attitudes towards teaching and learning (Morgan and Morris 1999). Our own work suggests that pupils of all ages value a teacher's sense of humour. Pupils in the early years of secondary schooling, when asked about their favourite teacher, highlight personality traits rather than pedagogical skills. In the GCSE years pupils stress the importance of a teacher's personality, as much as the strict adherence to a set of agreed rules, as a factor in keeping order in the classroom. So critical is this pupil affinity to teachers in facilitating effective learning that we have found that some pupils, by the end of Year 7, have hardened in their attitudes towards certain curriculum subjects because of the teachers who teach them: liking or disliking a subject has become dependent upon liking or disliking the teacher who teaches it.

Where teacher–pupil relations are good, it would appear easier for teachers to introduce an element of negotiation with pupils over the work to be done (Clarke 1991). A recent project, which tried to address the dip in academic performance of Year 8 pupils in eight Lincolnshire secondary schools, recognised the need to place pupil–teacher relationships on a firm footing by creating a dialogue that led to teachers giving pupils more responsibility in their schools and generally making them feel 'more special' (Homerton-Schools Research Circle 1999). From our own research, few schools appear to talk routinely with pupils about the work they should do. Where pupils are asked, it is our experience that they are very accepting of what is offered by teachers. In one IQEA school, which consulted its pupils on the curriculum on a regular basis, over two-thirds of a representative sample of pupils of all ages wanted no changes to the way that form tutorial periods were organised. Half of its Year 10 pupils wanted no changes in their general studies curriculum, and all but a handful of its Year 8 pupils could suggest no learning benefits of being able to go on-line in their homes, other than an increased access to the Internet.

Teachers under pressure to deliver the National Curriculum might shy away from opportunities to discuss with their pupils a less teacher-centred approach to curriculum planning. The lack of a range of options offered by pupils, where they are given an opportunity to contribute, suggests that there has been little classroom dialogue about different ways of teaching and learning. Pupils are therefore limited in the alternatives they can suggest by the boundaries imposed by their own learning experiences.

Pupils therefore seem to learn best when

- they get on well with teachers (Activity 4.1);
- they are motivated by teachers (Activity 4.2);
- they are helped by teachers (Activity 4.3);
- there is an element of negotiation with teachers over the work they should do (Activity 4.4).

Context

The importance to effective teaching and learning of teachers developing relationships with their pupils which show warmth, support and respect is well established. We have consistently maintained within IQEA that the responsibility for maintaining and developing such 'authentic relationships' lies firmly with the teachers themselves. It has always been a difficult task because pupils of different ages and genders have different views about the qualities that those they regard as 'good' teachers should possess. Nonetheless, fostering pupils' affinity with their teachers is of sufficient importance for teachers to seek ways of modifying their behaviour in lessons, in an effort to ensure that classes are not put off the process of learning.

Briefing

Aims

- To provide ways of obtaining information on the qualities that different groups of pupils value in their teachers.
- To promote discussion on ways in which teachers might improve pupils' affinity with them.

Process

This activity involves three stages. Step 1 involves collecting data on the qualities that different groups of pupils value in a teacher. In Step 2 the data are collated. Step 3 seeks to devise classroom strategies that address these views.

Step 1	You will want to collect the views of pupils in the classes that you teach. At the start of a lesson ask pupils to write down on paper the qualities of a good teacher. If this appears to be too abstract a task for some pupils, ask them to think of a good teacher (or teachers) they have had in the past, and to list what was good about them. Stress that they should not write their names above their lists, as it is intended to be an anonymous exercise. Collect in the sheets.

Step 2

Collate the data. Below are some data from a Nottinghamshire secondary school where a sample of 100 pupils were asked to define the characteristics of a good teacher. The qualities listed on the left are shown in rank order of popularity for Years 7, 8 and 9, with (B) indicating that a preponderance of boys gave the answer, (G) a preponderance of girls, and (BG) that there was no great preponderance of either.

Quality identified	Year 7	Year 8	Year 9
Funny	1 (BG)		=5 (BG)
Sense of humour	2 (B)	4 (G)	2 (BG)
Pleasant	=3 (G)	=5 (BG)	=5 (G)
Helpful	=3 (G)	2 (BG)	=5 (G)
Provides fun lesson activities	=3 (B)	=5 (BG)	3 (B)
Explains well	=3 (BG)		
Approachable	7 (G)	3 (G)	
'In tune with' pupils		1 (B)	1 (BG)
Provides range of learning activities		=5 (BG)	
Understanding			4 (BG)
Provides element of pupil choice			=5 (G)

As with these responses, your list might well contain qualities that relate more to the personalities of teachers than to specific teaching skills.

Step 3

Step 3 is to discuss with another colleague if and how you can modify your own classroom behaviour to accommodate some of the qualities highlighted by the pupils. Regarding the data in Step 2, you might ask the following questions.

- Do I need to spend a little time with my Year 8 and Year 9 classes talking about how they spend their spare time?
- What do my pupils mean by 'fun activities', and can I introduce more without affecting the pace of my lessons?
- Am I too strict in reacting to comments and asides that pupils regard as witty?
- Do I get around my Year 7 classes enough to find out what learning problems they might have?

© John Beresford 2003 – Creating the Conditions to Involve Pupils in Their Learning

Activity 4.2: motivation to work

Context

Getting on well with teachers is an important element in the motivation of pupils to work hard and to produce good work. There are a number of discrete teacher behaviours that can also influence levels of pupil motivation (see Hopkins *et al.* 1997: 17). There is a range of other factors and attitudes towards work, about which teachers might be less aware, that also affects pupil motivation.

Briefing

Aims

- To provide a schedule for teachers to assess the relative importance of various factors and attitudes in motivating pupils in the classroom.
- To adjust classroom practice in response to these findings.

Process

This schedule is part of a larger questionnaire that has been used successfully in a large Essex secondary school to find out the views of nearly 600 Year 7 and Year 8 pupils on aspects of teaching and learning. Teachers can amend the schedule if they wish, to accommodate the practices in their own schools. The activity is organised into three steps. Step 1 involves administering the schedule. It takes less than five minutes to complete, and is ideally suited to being completed in a registration or tutorial session. In Step 2, the data is collated and analysed. A method of analysis is offered. Thereafter, in Step 3, you might want to review your current classroom practice in the light of the findings, and if necessary adjust certain aspects accordingly.

Step 1   The questionnaire takes only a short time for pupils to complete. You can change or add to the statements to reflect your own ways of working within the school.

WHAT MAKES YOU WANT TO WORK HARD?

The teachers in the school are interested in what it is about particular lessons that makes you want to work hard and to the best of your ability in them. Please fill in the following questionnaire. **We do not need to know your name.**

I AM IN CLASS _____   I AM A   BOY   GIRL

(please circle the correct answer)

Please circle which of the four words after each of the following statements best reflects your feelings.

I work to the best of my ability when:

(a) I'm interested in the subject	RARELY	SOMETIMES	OFTEN	ALWAYS
(b) I see the subject as important	RARELY	SOMETIMES	OFTEN	ALWAYS
(c) I like the teacher	RARELY	SOMETIMES	OFTEN	ALWAYS
(d) The teacher explains tasks clearly	RARELY	SOMETIMES	OFTEN	ALWAYS
(e) The teacher expects me to work hard	RARELY	SOMETIMES	OFTEN	ALWAYS
(f) My work is praised	RARELY	SOMETIMES	OFTEN	ALWAYS

Thank you for filling in this questionnaire.

 © *John Beresford 2003 – Creating the Conditions to Involve Pupils in Their Learning*

Step 2

You now need to collate and analyse the data. By scoring 'Rarely' responses for each statement as 1, 'Sometimes' as 2, 'Often' 3 and 'Always' 4, and then working out the average score for each statement for each gender-group in each year-group to whom you have administered the questionnaire, you can get an at-a-glance assessment of the comparative weightings of each of the six factors listed. Scores above 3.0 indicate high preference levels. Below are data collected from the Essex school that used the schedule.

	Average scores for each statement			
I work to the best of my ability when:	Year 7 boys	Year 7 girls	Year 8 boys	Year 8 girls
I'm interested in the subject	3.4	3.5	3.4	3.5
I see the subject as important	2.9	3.0	3.0	3.0
I like the teacher	2.7	3.0	2.7	2.9
The teacher explains tasks clearly	2.9	3.2	3.1	3.2
The teacher expects me to work hard	3.2	3.2	3.0	3.0
My work is praised	2.6	2.7	2.8	2.8

All the listed factors have ratings above 2.5, which suggests that pupils in the school see all six factors as quite important in getting them to work hard. Subject interest is the most important factor for all four groups. Teacher expectations are important to Year 7 pupils, and teachers' ability to explain scores highly with Year 7 girls and Year 8 pupils. However, making subjects interesting is clearly the key factor in establishing and maintaining pupil motivation in the school.

Step 3

You will now want to review your own classroom practice in the light of the responses given by your own pupils. You may find the following questions useful.

- How do I gauge the interest of pupils in a subject?
- Do I justify the content of each lesson that I teach as a matter of course?
- Do I have the personal qualities that enable me to get on with my pupils? (See Activity 4.1.)
- Do I spend sufficient time checking the understanding of the pupils?
- Do I express my work expectations clearly to pupils?
- How do I praise pupils?

Activity 4.3: being helpful to pupils

Context

Teachers who have the personal qualities valued by pupils tend to create a classroom climate in which pupils are more prepared to approach them for help with their work. Teachers often rely upon their personal knowledge of the pupils to gauge the nature and quantity of the help they are prepared to give. However, in some circumstances it can be useful to reflect upon what practices pupils as a group have found useful in the past. One of these circumstances is preparation for examinations.

Briefing

Aims

- To provide a schedule to enable pupils to evaluate the support given in preparation for examinations.
- To provide teachers with data to modify, if necessary, the nature of the support they give.

Process

The schedule provided is one used in a Cambridgeshire secondary school to evaluate the support given to a group of Year 10 pupils who had just sat their 'mock' examinations. In this instance, pupils were interviewed singly. The activity comprises three steps. Step 1 gives teachers the opportunity to adapt the set of questions provided, to suit the purposes of the school. Step 2 involves organising the interviews. Pupils will be less inhibited in their responses if the interviews are conducted by someone who does not teach them. The purpose of Step 3 is to analyse the findings, and, if necessary, to modify the nature of the support given to pupils in future years.

 © John Beresford 2003 – Creating the Conditions to Involve Pupils in Their Learning

Step 1   You might choose to modify the schedule below in order to accommodate your own practices and particular needs.

Interview schedule to evaluate the support given to Year 10 pupils in preparing for their 'mock' examinations

1. What were the Year 10 exams like?
   How did you do?

2. Did you feel well prepared?
   Who helped you?

3. How much *extra* work did you do in preparation?

4. Were you given any advice on how to revise?
   What did you find most useful?

5. What feedback did you get on your exam performance?
   Was it useful?

6. How do you feel about your chances in the GCSE exams now?

7. Do you think you will change your approach to working, at school or at home?

8. Has it been useful to have exams in Year 10?
   Why?

Step 2   The original interviews that took place in the Cambridgeshire secondary school were conducted by someone not known to the pupils. Pupils were interviewed singly, although you may prefer them to be interviewed in groups.

Step 3   You now need to analyse the findings and to modify, if necessary, the practices you use to support pupils who are preparing for examinations. Pupils in the original interviews said that they found the provision of revision plans by teachers and the working through of past papers in classwork sessions to be very useful. The widespread use of parents by pupils in their revision suggested that parents might also appreciate some guidance on the kinds of questions to ask their children.

Activity 4.4: discussing with pupils the work to be done

Context

With the increasing levels of national prescription as to what should be taught in schools, there are limited opportunities for teachers to negotiate with their pupils over what work should be done in lessons. However, pupils having some such say in the curriculum they receive is an important element in providing the sense of ownership over their learning that is crucial in the development of pupils' learning autonomy, and in the acquisition of the good learning habits necessary for lifelong learning.

Briefing

Aims

- To provide a questionnaire for pupils to evaluate and suggest modifications to a subject curriculum.
- To provide teachers with data that can be used, if necessary, in the modification of the curriculum taught to their pupils.

Process

The schedule accompanying this activity was used by teachers in a boys' comprehensive school in north Hertfordshire to canvass the views of pupils in Years 10 and 11 on the general studies course they were currently undertaking. The school opted to use a questionnaire because it wanted to canvass as many pupils as possible. There are four steps to follow in this activity. Step 1 involves adjusting the questionnaire to the needs of the school or of the subject teachers. The questionnaire is then administered in Step 2, and Step 3 engages teachers in analysing the results. Step 4 provides an opportunity to review the curriculum in its current state and to modify it, where appropriate, in the light of pupils' comments.

© John Beresford 2003 – Creating the Conditions to Involve Pupils in Their Learning

Step 1   You will need to modify the questionnaire to suit your own needs, the needs of your department or the needs of your school.

Step 2   The school that originally administered this particular questionnaire felt that the best place to do so was during a general studies lesson, when teachers could explain more fully the reason behind the exercise. With other members of staff, decide where best to administer your questionnaire.

HOW DO YOU FEEL ABOUT GENERAL STUDIES?

Please respond to the questions below as fully as you can. Your answers will help the staff to develop and improve the general studies course in the school. **We do not need to know your name.**

I AM IN YEAR GROUP _____

1. How much do you enjoy general studies?   1   2   3   4   5
    (1 = not at all; 5 = very much) (circle correct number)

2. Do you think it is an important school subject?   1   2   3   4   5
    (1 = not at all; 5 = very much) (circle correct number)

3. What are the reasons for your answers to Questions 1 and 2?

4. What have you enjoyed most in general studies in the last two terms?

    Why did you enjoy this in particular?

5. What in your view has been the most **important** subject you have studied in general studies?

6. What have you enjoyed least?

    What was the reason?

7. Which skills do you feel you have learned over the past two terms (for example, how to work in a team)?

8. Are there other skills you would like to learn about in general studies?

    What are they?

9. Are there any subjects you would like to learn about in general studies?

    What are they?

    Why do you think they should be included in the programme?

10. Is there anything that can be done to make general studies better for you?

    Thank you for filling in this questionnaire.

Step 3

Once the questionnaires have been completed, you need to analyse the results. Questions 1 and 2 are best analysed by scoring each of the responses according to the number circled, and working out an average for each of the cohorts – in the sample school's case this is for Year 10 and Year 11 pupils (if you want to find out gender differences, you will need to insert an appropriate question in the schedule).

Step 4

You will now need to review the curriculum you are currently teaching in the light of pupils' comments and, if it is appropriate, to make modifications. The findings of the north Hertfordshire school's survey led staff to review the school's policy of using outside speakers (which pupils generally disliked), to consider replacing one topic that pupils felt covered 'old ground' with another that a number of pupils had advocated, and to consider introducing more work that could be done in small groups, increasing the amount that teachers had employed in the previous year.

© *John Beresford 2003 – Creating the Conditions to Involve Pupils in Their Learning*

CHAPTER 5

Learning repertoire

There is a considerable body of research knowledge (see, for example, Brophy and Good 1986; Joyce and Weil 1986; Joyce *et al.* 1987) that supports our fundamental belief within the IQEA project that an extensive teaching repertoire is one of the key classroom conditions necessary for school improvement to take place (West *et al.* 1995; Hopkins *et al.* 1997; Hopkins *et al.* 1998).

There is already an extensive literature on the component parts of effective teaching (see, for example, Rosenshine and Stevens 1986; Gipps 1992; Harris 1995), but less on the process of matching teaching strategies to pupils' learning styles. There have been a number of instruments designed, mainly in the form of questionnaires or interview schedules, to try to discover the learning preferences of discrete groups of pupils: of secondary science pupils (Cunliffe 1995), for pupils excluded from school (De Pear 1997), for eight- to eleven-year-olds (Norwich 1998) and for Year 10 pupils (Barnett 1985). The VAK (visual/auditory/kinaesthetic) analysis of how pupils process information is now used in many schools. However, much of the matching of teaching and learning styles has been extremely speculative, based upon the premise that if a sufficient variety of strategies is employed, then a catch-all effect will apply: 'By offering a range of learning opportunities, including those that use their strengths, teachers are more likely to provide a learning experience that pupils feel good about' (Faccenda and Fielding 1992). As Joyce *et al.* (1997: 15) similarly state: 'Increasing the range of learning experiences provided in our schools increases the likelihood of more pupils becoming more adept learners.'

The need for some form of dialogue between teachers and pupils about teaching and learning methods in the classroom has been recognised by a number of writers (see, for example, Levin 1994; Hord 1997; Hubbard 1997) and, increasingly, by a number of the schools in the IQEA project. These schools have shown themselves willing to canvass pupils on their views about what constitutes effective teaching.

Using an observation schedule derived from the work of Kolb (1984) and its application to classroom activities (Fielding 1994), we have undertaken a series of lesson observations across a wide range of schools (including, of late, primary schools) and school subjects over the past five or so years. For the purposes of the research, the 38 listed classroom activities were divided into four categories to correspond to Kolb's learning style categories:

- sensing/doing activities (accommodative), like simulations;
- thinking/watching activities (assimilative), like teacher demonstrations;
- thinking/doing activities (convergent), like note-taking;
- sensing/watching activities (divergent), like discussions.

At the same time we have used an elaborated version of the schedule to canvass pupil learning preferences. A fuller exposition of the methodology and research appears elsewhere (Beresford 1999c). The strategies, along with their categories, are reproduced as part of Activity 5.1.

We used data from 74 lessons observed in eight secondary schools. The number of different strategies and activities used in the lessons observed ranged from 7 to 23. The lesson profiles showed a reasonable balance between doing and watching orientations in all of the subject categories, but a marked imbalance between sensing and thinking orientations except in drama and a few other isolated lessons.

The combined data suggested a quite stunning uniformity of teaching diet in the classrooms of the eight schools. Art and music teachers were employing the same activities and strategies as science, English and French teachers. Each school, irrespective of its catchment area and examination performance, catered overwhelmingly for pupils with convergent and assimilative learning styles. It would appear that most of the teachers observed in the 74 lessons relied upon a restricted repertoire characterised by largely didactic teaching methods, a reliance confirmed in the research of others (Hacker and Carter 1987; Newton and Harwood 1993).

While pupils' learning preferences showed a bias towards assimilative and convergent activities, they demonstrated a desire for a far greater proportion of accommodative and divergent activities than their teachers were offering. Three schools offered their pupils a diet of four parts convergent and assimilative activities to one part accommodative and divergent: their pupils stated a group preference for a 3 : 2 ratio. Another school offered a 9 : 1 ratio of similar activities: their pupils, with an interesting conservatism compared to their peers in the three other schools, preferred a 2 : 1 ratio.

The instrument was created with the intention of providing schools with a broadbrush picture of the teaching activities and strategies used by teachers, and of the learning preferences of their pupils. The derived data were intended to provide a focus for a discussion among the staff and, perhaps, between staff and pupils about teaching methods. This has generally been the case. In one school, for example, the results confirmed staff's fears about the lack of opportunities provided for independent learning in its 11–16 classes, a lack which they felt partly explained their comparatively disappointing 'A' level results. The school has since provided more of these activities, including cooperative group learning, and has been provided with audit sheets in order to monitor whether such learning is taking place. The community studies department in another school has tried to integrate more accommodative and divergent activities into its curriculum, and has involved pupils in evaluating the activities (see Beresford 1998b). In yet another, teachers have learned how to organise inductive learning sessions using paired and groupwork techniques, and have involved staff and pupils in an evaluation of the effectiveness of the teaching model. In each of these schools, pupils were coached in the various learning strategies necessary to take full advantage of the teaching strategies and models that their teachers were developing.

Pupils seem to learn best when

- teachers use a variety of teaching styles and strategies (Activity 5.1);
- pupils are equipped to cope with the range of teaching styles and strategies used (Activity 5.2);
- pupils find lessons interesting (Activity 5.3);
- pupils are taught new ways of working and learning (Activity 5.4).

Activity 5.1: building variety into lessons

Context

Teachers who provide a range of teaching strategies in their lessons help to develop their pupils' learning capacities in a number of ways. Where they use such a range, teachers are likely to engage greater numbers of their pupils in the learning process than if they restrict themselves, for example, to strategies associated with didactic teaching. Their pupils are also more likely to develop as versatile learners who are able to take advantage of a range of learning activities. Providing a range of activities can also lessen classroom disruption, and can motivate pupils.

Briefing

Aims

- To provide a broadbrush planning document as a checklist for teachers seeking to build variety into their lessons.
- To provide an instrument for pupils to feed back on the variety perceived in lessons they have attended.

Process

Although originally intended as an observation schedule (see Beresford 1998a: 30–4; Beresford 1999b; Hopkins 2001: 21–4; 2002: 129–32), the accompanying checklist of planned teaching strategies has been used by teachers in a south Essex comprehensive school as a planning document. They periodically fill it in before lessons to check that they are providing a range of teaching activities. The second schedule, designed for pupils, is also intended for periodic use, perhaps at the end of a week's teaching or at the end of a particular subject module. There are three steps to this activity. Step 1 is intended to help teachers to decide how often they will undertake this self-checking exercise. Once they have decided, they tick each of the strategies they plan to use in a particular lesson. Having done this for a number of lessons, Step 2 invites them to compare sheets to determine whether they are providing a range of teaching strategies in a particular class over a period of time. In Step 3 teachers match their own assessments with those of their pupils by administering the pupil schedule.

© John Beresford 2003 – Creating the Conditions to Involve Pupils in Their Learning

Step 1

The first schedule lists 38 commonly used teaching strategies, classified according to Kolb's four identified learning styles (for further information on the rationale behind the schedule, you need to consult the works referenced on the previous page). 'Ac' refers to accommodative activities, 'As' to assimilative, 'C' to convergent and 'D' to divergent. A lesson that caters predominantly for accommodative learners would typically allow children to experiment with various materials with minimal intervention from the teacher. Similarly, a predominantly divergent lesson would require the teacher to facilitate group discussion on an issue. Both of these types of lesson cater primarily for social learning. In a predominantly assimilative lesson students might listen while the teacher talks on a topic from the front of the class. In a convergent-type lesson students work alone applying acquired skills to practical activities, for example solving mathematical problems. Both of the latter two lessons generally involve students working alone, and incorporate a high degree of didactic teaching.

This schedule is intended to provide you with a quick checklist of which strategies you have planned to use in a particular lesson, and to indicate which learning styles they cater for. You might want to use it for every lesson, for every lesson with a particular class, or occasionally over a longer period of time. Tick each strategy you have planned to use, and then add up the ticks for each learning style and total them in the appropriate boxes (Ac, D, C, As) at the bottom of the sheet. If nearly all of your ticks have been for C and As activities, the lesson is predominantly didactic. If there are numbers of ticks for Ac and D, the lesson is more pupil-centred. If you have more ticks for Ac and C combined than for D and As combined, the lesson will contain more active than passive learning activities.

Step 2

Compare sheets for a series of lessons. You should be aiming for ticks in all the boxes over a period of time if you intend to provide a range of teaching strategies to accommodate all types of learning and learners.

Step 3

Administer the pupils' 'Teaching Activities' schedule in order to match their assessments with yours.

Checklist of planned teaching strategies

Date: Lesson:

Teaching strategies		Incidence
Accuracy stressed	C	
Accurate recall	As	
Action planning	As	
Brainstorming	D	
Case study	As	
Choice of activities	C	
Classwork	As	
Clear goals expressed	C	
Comprehension	C	
Data collection	As	
Demonstrations	As	
Discussion	D	
Group interaction	D	
Groupwork organised	Ac	
Gut feelings asked for	Ac	
Hand-outs	As	
Investigations	D	
Lecture	As	
Mistakes allowed	Ac	
Note-taking	C	
Open-ended questions asked	D	
Paired work	D	
Planning of work by pupils	C	
Practising skills	C	
Problem-solving	C	
Reflection on experience	D	
Relevance of work explained	C	
Reporting back methods varied	Ac	
Role play	D	
Scientific experiments	C	
Simulations used	Ac	
Specialisms tapped	As	
Testing	C	
Thoroughness stressed	C	
Variety of approaches	Ac	
Video	As	
Working alone	C, As	
Worksheets	C	

Ac		D	
C		As	

© *John Beresford 2003 – Creating the Conditions to Involve Pupils in Their Learning*

Teaching Activities

Please tick which activities you have had in lessons over the past_____

in _____

Description of activity	
One where accuracy is important	
One where I'm asked to recall information accurately	
One where the teacher involves me and the class in the planning of our work	
One where we are asked to brainstorm ideas and facts	
One where we look at case studies and other real-life examples	
One where we are given a choice of activities to learn the same thing	
One where we are taught as a class, and all do the same work	
One where the teacher makes the goals of the lesson clear	
One where we have to interpret information given to us	
One where we have to collect information and data ourselves	
One where the teacher demonstrates something	
One where we have a group or class discussion	
One where we can work things out in groups	
One where the teacher organises groupwork	
One where the teacher asks us for our feelings about something	
One where the teacher gives us information on printed sheets	
One where we have to undertake investigations	
One where the teacher gives us information through teaching in front of the class	
One where I'm allowed to make mistakes	
One where I take notes	
One where lots of different answers are possible	
One where I work in pairs	
One where I plan my own work	
One where we practise skills	
One where we have to solve a problem	
One where I'm asked to think about my experiences	
One where the reason I'm doing something is clear to me	
One where we can report back our findings in different ways	
One where we have role play	
One where we do experiments	
One where we have to deal with simulated, real-life situations	
One where I can use my particular skills	
One where we are being tested	
One where I have to be thorough and careful in my work	
One where the teacher uses different teaching methods	
One where we have a video	
One where I work alone	
One where worksheets are given out	

I am in Year _____   I am male / female
                                          (circle correct one)

Thank you for filling in this questionnaire.

© John Beresford 2003 – Creating the Conditions to Involve Pupils in Their Learning

Activity 5.2: coping with different teaching styles

Context

Teachers who use a range of teaching activities and models provide a range of learning activities for their pupils. Pupils, however, might not necessarily have acquired the learning skills to take full advantage of such a range. Teachers, for example, might provide a number of cooperative learning opportunities in their lessons, but their pupils might not have the social and learning skills necessary to work effectively in groups. An element of coaching might be necessary, and teachers might need to be vigilant in order to ensure that classes are benefiting fully from the teaching approaches on offer.

Briefing

Aim

- To provide an interview schedule that gives teachers feedback on how well their pupils are coping with a new teaching model.

Process

This schedule has been used in a Derbyshire secondary school that introduced inductive teaching into their curriculum (see Hopkins and Harris 2000, chapter 5 for a description of the introduction and an explanation of what inductive teaching entails). It was used after the inductive teaching process had been extensively used over a period of months across the whole range of subjects taught in the school. The activity consists of three steps. Step 1 invites teachers to adapt the accompanying schedule for the strategies or teaching models that they wish pupils to evaluate. Step 2 involves organising the interviews. These are best conducted by someone who does not teach the pupils. In Step 3, the findings are examined with a view to refining the future use of the particular teaching model.

© *John Beresford 2003 – Creating the Conditions to Involve Pupils in Their Learning*

Step 1   Unless you are asking pupils for their comments on inductive teaching, you should amend the interview schedule below to meet your own purposes.

Interview schedule for evaluation of inductive teaching by pupils

1. Do you enjoy inductive teaching? (*Prompt if necessary*)
    Do the rest of your classmates enjoy it?
    Is it preferable to other ways of teaching?
    Why?

2. Can you describe what inductive teaching involves?
    What do you have to do?
    Is it used in the same way in all subjects?

3. Which parts did you find hard?
    Which parts did other students find hard?

4. Do you think you have learnt more in inductive lessons?
    How can you tell?
    Which parts helped you to learn and understand better?
    In which lessons has it been most useful?

5. Has inductive teaching encouraged you to use the techniques in lessons not taught inductively?

© John Beresford 2003 – Creating the Conditions to Involve Pupils in Their Learning   61

UNIVERSITY OF HERTFORDSHIRE LRC

Step 2   You now need to organise the interviews. In the Derbyshire school where the schedule was first used, interviews were conducted by someone who did not teach any of the pupils. Pupils can be interviewed singly, in pairs or in groups.

Step 3   You should now examine the findings of the interviews with a view to refining the teaching practices associated with the particular teaching model. The pupils in the Derbyshire school acknowledged that the inductive learning was an extremely useful addition to their learning repertoires, and that they enjoyed and were motivated by the learning processes involved. However, they highlighted in their comments the problem of absent pupils 'catching up' with a process that often took two or three lessons to complete, and staff integrated appropriate procedures into inductive lessons in order to address this.

   © John Beresford 2003 – Creating the Conditions to Involve Pupils in Their Learning

Activity 5.3: making lessons interesting

Context

Teachers who provide a range of learning activities that pupils can both enjoy and engage with contribute significantly to pupils' learning capacities. Lessons that pupils find interesting improve pupil learning because they not only engage students but also motivate them to work harder and to work well. Pupils who find lessons interesting tend not to join in with disruptive activity. Finding out what pupils find interesting should be a key factor in teacher planning.

Briefing

Aim

- To suggest an activity that teachers can stage with their classes to determine what pupils think makes a lesson interesting.

Process

Just as Activity 4.1 addressed the qualities of those whom pupils regarded as good teachers, this activity addresses the qualities of what pupils regard as interesting lessons. It is divided into three parts. Step 1 invites the class to write down what they think makes a good lesson. As a prompt, teachers can ask pupils to think of interesting lessons they have recently been taught, and to jot down what was good about them. Step 2 involves the collation of data, and Step 3 gives teachers the chance to modify, if necessary, lesson planning to accommodate pupils' views.

Step 1   The activity can be done at the beginning or end of a lesson. Invite pupils to think about what makes a lesson interesting. As a prompt you can ask them to think of some interesting lessons they have recently been taught, and to write down in a list what made them interesting. For richer data you might also ask them what makes a lesson uninteresting, using the same prompts.

Step 2   You now need to collate and analyse the data. Pupils in a Nottinghamshire secondary school came up with the following lists of features that made for interesting and uninteresting lessons. The features are presented in rank order.

Interesting lessons have . . .	*Uninteresting lessons have . . .*
An element of activity, or games	Pupils misbehaving
Active pupil involvement	Teacher shouting
An element of fun	Copying from the board
Good teacher explanation	Repeated work
Help for individuals from the teacher	Whole-class punishments
Discussion	Too much teacher talk
Cordial pupil-teacher relations	Poor teacher explanation
Learning something new	Poor class control by teacher
An element of ICT	Feeling 'put on the spot'
Being allowed to 'get on' with work	Unchallenging work

Step 3   You will now want to review your classroom practice in the light of the findings from the activity. The Nottinghamshire school noted both the importance of support for pupils in completing work tasks in class, and the importance of keeping adequate class control, not only to engage those who were being disruptive but also for the benefit of those who were not involved in disruptive behaviour.

   © John Beresford 2003 – Creating the Conditions to Involve Pupils in Their Learning

Activity 5.4: being taught new ways of working

Context

It was suggested in Activity 3.3 that teachers might have to coach their classes in the social skills necessary to make collaborative groupwork an effective learning strategy. It will also be necessary, for example for most of the teaching models described in *Creating the Conditions for Teaching and Learning* (Hopkins and Harris 2000), to instruct and give repeated practice to pupils in the learning techniques involved. Although pupils may have had some experience of working in groups, they may not necessarily possess the knowledge of how best to organise collaborative learning activities. For many pupils, learning inductively might be a new experience, and teachers may be required to model inductive learning activities on a number of occasions before pupils become proficient in the techniques involved.

Briefing

Aim

• To provide teachers with observation templates to assess how well their pupils have assimilated the learning techniques associated with collaborative groupwork and inductive teaching.

Process

The two observation schedules reproduced below have been used in primary and secondary schools where teachers have coached pupils in the social and organisational skills required to take full advantage of each of the models of learning. They are designed for use by teachers to evaluate how well pupils have grasped the principles and techniques associated with the particular models of learning. Teachers who are clear on the steps pupils need to take in order to benefit fully from other models, for example whole-class teaching, will be able to devise their own observation schedules.

This activity is organised into two stages. In Step 1, preparations for the observation are made. Because the collaborative groupwork and inductive teaching models involve a great deal of independent pupil activity and learning, teachers can be free for long periods during lessons and may use the time to undertake observations. Pupils should be informed of the purpose of the observation. Where pupils are being observed during sessions that require the ongoing involvement of teachers, for example whole-class teaching, a learning assistant who is familiar with the schedule could be asked to observe.

Step 2 involves reviewing the notes taken during the observation, with a view to addressing any perceived shortcomings in the skills and techniques noted during the learning activity.

Step 1   You should become familiar with the schedule before you undertake the observation. The schedules reproduced describe the steps in which the pupils in the various schools were coached to take full advantage of the learning activity. You might want to amend the schedules. If you wish to draw up your own schedule for another teaching model that you use frequently, for example whole-class teaching, you need to be clear yourself on the steps pupils need to follow in order for them to participate fully. You may find *Creating the Conditions for Teaching and Learning* (Hopkins and Harris 2000) useful in this respect, chapter 3 of which deals with whole-class teaching.

Once you have become familiar with the schedule, you can undertake an observation. You will find that you have long periods during inductive and groupwork activities where pupils will be working independently, and in such cases you will have time to do the observation yourself. Where you are more actively involved, for example in whole-class teaching, you may need to ask a learning assistant who is familiar with the schedule to undertake an observation. Pupils should be made aware of the purpose of the observation.

Step 2   Once the observation has been completed, you will want to review the notes that you or another observer have made. The findings might highlight areas where the learning process could be improved, which might necessitate further coaching and practice in those skills and techniques.

© John Beresford 2003 – Creating the Conditions to Involve Pupils in Their Learning

OBSERVATION SCHEDULE FOR COOPERATIVE DISCIPLINED ENQUIRY

Class: _____ Subject: _____

Lesson Incidents	Yes	No	Notes
Introduction			
Teacher selects work groupings			
Pupils select work groupings			
Cooperative tasks allocated to groups			
Pupils are clear about the task allocated			
Groupwork			
Pupils cooperate in task:			
• Regulate their own behaviour			
• Select a leader			
• Divide the labour			
• Keep on-task			
• Take turns			
Plenary session			
Groups are able to articulate findings			

Source: Joyce, B., Calhoun, E. and Hopkins, D. (1997) *Models of Learning – Tools for Teaching.* Buckingham: Open University Press.

OBSERVATION SCHEDULE FOR INDUCTIVE TEACHING AND LEARNING

Class: _____ Subject: _____

Lesson Incidents	Yes	No	Notes
Introduction			
Teacher outlines lesson objectives			
Teacher designates work groups			
Teacher presents data sets			
Pupils collect own data sets			
Classifying and labelling data			
Teacher sets boundaries for classification			
Pupils understand criteria and procedures for classification			
Pupils work on their own			
Pupils work in pairs			
Pupils work in groups			
The exercise is done as a class activity			
Plenary session			
Pupils are able to explain attributes			
Pupils are able to provide names for categories			
Teacher explores cause and effect relationships with pupils			
Pupils are able to draw inferences and conclusions about data			
Teacher asks predictive questions: 'What would happen if . . . ?'			
Pupils are able to make predictions			
Pupils can explain reasons for their predictions			
Teacher designates follow-up activities			

Source: Joyce, B., Calhoun, E. and Hopkins, D. (1997) *Models of Learning – Tools for Teaching.* Buckingham: Open University Press.

© John Beresford 2003 – Creating the Conditions to Involve Pupils in Their Learning

CHAPTER 6

Orientation to learning

Pedagogic partnerships describe a series of arrangements in schools whereby teachers are able to learn or disseminate proven teaching practices with the help of a critical friend. In seeking to develop this particular condition in schools we have leant heavily in the project upon the work of Joyce (see, for example, Joyce and Weil 1986; Joyce *et al.* 1997), and have promoted the use of such staff development techniques as peer coaching and modelling. In this way we have subscribed to the view that 'in a community of learners, the most important role of teacher and principal is that of head learner' (Barth 1996). We believe that pupil learning is enhanced when this commitment to learning is shared by the pupils themselves.

Most of the pupils we talk to want to do well in school. The majority, though a greater proportion of girls than boys, also believe that they work hard. Despite research which suggests that they learn better outside school (see, for example, Shaughnessy and Kushman 1997), most feel they do most of their learning in school. Those most satisfied with school are high achievers who feel motivated and esteemed for their work (Epstein and McPartland 1976). Those least satisfied are those who find certain subjects difficult, feel that teachers do not help them in their difficulties or have developed 'learned helplessness' in work they find hard to understand (Chaplain 1996a; 1996b; Galloway *et al.* 1995). Pupils as young as five and six have apparently developed the concept of specific subject competence, and ascribe their success to this and to personal effort (which their teachers' comments confirm), rather than to all-round ability (Gipps and Tunstall 1997). Pupils' perceptions of their own ability in particular subjects appear to persist into the first year of secondary school, but decline thereafter (Keys and Fernandes 1993). This decline has in part been used to explain the Year 8 'dip' in pupil performance (Meece and Miller 1996; Rudduck and Flutter 1998) and for the decline in pupils' positive attitudes towards all curriculum subjects except English in Key Stage 3 (Sutcliffe 1998; MORI/Campaign For Learning 1998; Miller *et al.* 1999). Within IQEA we have also found that pupils as early as their first year of secondary education assess the importance of some subjects in terms of how it will help them secure future employment.

We have suggested above that teachers can do much to modify pupils' attitudes towards specific curriculum subjects. They can, for example, deploy a range of teaching strategies to make their lessons more interesting. They can build an 'authentic relationship' with those they teach so that pupils do not equate 'doing badly' with not getting along with the subject teacher. They can emphasise task performance criteria in feedback to pupils, rather than concentrating solely on building (or lowering) self-esteem. The instrumental attitude of many pupils to school work has led us to suggest to some of our IQEA schools that subject teachers routinely justify to their pupils why their subjects are part of the school curriculum. We also feel it is important to explain the relevance, as well as the aims and objectives, of lessons. It is also our experience that many teachers do not explain the relevance of homework tasks in improving and extending pupils' learning. Consequently, we have found that some pupils feel embittered that homework impinges unfairly upon their free time, particularly where they cannot see the point of a specific task that they have been set.

In terms of motivating pupils, our own experiences of the various merit systems operating in schools is that they are successful in the first year of secondary school, less successful in the following year and that they have generally lost their currency by the end of Year 9. A number of Year 9 pupils recognise that teachers give an excessive number of such rewards to younger pupils in order to stimulate effort. Target-setting has some reported motivational effects (Perkins 1999), although some pupils have felt that schools are more concerned with enhancing institutional performance than with the development of the individual (Boyd and Jardine 1997; Fielding 1999). GCSE work and assessment provide its own motivation for most pupils, and those who are alienated from work for public examinations are often alienated by their peers (Rudduck 1996a; 1996b).

Pupils appear more ready to learn when

- they look forward to lessons (Activity 6.1);
- they work hard in school (Activity 6.2);
- they work hard at homework (Activity 6.3);
- they feel that their hard work is acknowledged by teachers (Activity 6.4).

Activity 6.1: looking forward to lessons

Context

Preparing pupils for lifelong learning involves developing a positive orientation in them towards learning. This positive orientation entails a commitment to learning, a willingness as well as an ability to seek out and benefit from learning opportunities. Pupils have favourite subjects, and exploring further with pupils what it is that makes them like particular areas of learning might provide teachers with clues as to how they can foster such a positive orientation in other subjects.

Briefing

Aim

- To determine pupils' favourite subjects, and what it is about those subjects that makes pupils like them.

Process

Because identifying the features of favourite lessons might be regarded by teachers and pupils as a less 'threatening' activity than identifying the qualities of 'good' teachers and 'good' lessons, this activity can be undertaken in an open, whole-class session. It might be appropriate to do the activity in the first few days of pupils starting a new stage in their school careers, for example entering the junior department in a primary school or starting secondary school, before attitudes towards subjects become more fixed. The activity consists of five steps. In Step 1, teachers ask pupils if they have favourite subjects. These can be listed on the board. Step 2 asks pupils to think carefully about what it is that makes these subjects their favourites. Pupils might discuss this at length with a partner before reporting back to the whole class. In Step 3, the features that pupils identify are listed on the board and then the implications of the list are rehearsed with the class in Step 4. Step 5 gives practitioners the opportunity to share the list with teaching colleagues, and to discuss with them the implications for the planning of their teaching.

Step 1	In a class session, ask pupils to tell you their favourite subjects. List them on the board.
Step 2	Now ask pupils to think carefully about what it is that makes these subjects their favourites. Give pupils time to discuss this in pairs.
Step 3	On the board, list the features identified by pupils. Below are the most common responses of a group of Year 10 pupils in a Derbyshire comprehensive school who were asked the question near the beginning of their GCSE final year:

Enjoyment of, and interest in, the subject
Good teacher explanation
Teacher modelling answers
Teacher providing help for individuals
Lessons involve lots of activity
Lessons involve lots of writing
Teaching is challenging and motivational
Teaching is good

Step 4	You will now want to rehearse the implications of their responses with the class. The teacher of the Year 10 Derbyshire pupils might have asked the questions below.

- What is your attitude to an important core subject that you may find uninteresting?
- What would you do if you were taught your favourite subject by a teacher you didn't get on with?
- Do you accept that some learning in certain subjects might not entail a lot of activity/writing?

Step 5	Colleagues might be interested in sharing the pupils' list of features with you and in discussing the implications for the planning of learning activities in their own subjects.

   © John Beresford 2003 – Creating the Conditions to Involve Pupils in Their Learning

Activity 6.2: working hard

Context

Pupils who have developed the skills of autonomous learners and who have a positive orientation towards work will be aware of the effort they have to apply in order to complete work tasks. Those pupils developing these skills will benefit from some form of collective review of what 'hard work' entails, a review that includes the views of teachers as well as pupils. Arriving at some sort of consensus establishes common criteria to which both teachers and pupils can refer.

Briefing

Aim

• To provide an activity through which pupils and their teacher can achieve some consensus on what constitutes 'hard work'.

Process

Like Activity 6.1, this exercise is best undertaken at the beginning of a new phase of pupils' education, when views on subjects and hard work are likely to be more 'liquid'. This four-stage activity is best conducted as an open, whole-class exercise. Step 1 involves finding out how many pupils think that they work hard in school. Step 2 is a brainstorming session in which pupils consider how they know they are working hard. In Step 3, their views are collated and compared with those of the teacher. Step 4 seeks to arrive at some common understanding.

Step 1

Ask the pupils in your class how many of them think they work hard in school. From experience, most will put up their hands. Confirm with those that don't respond that they work hard sometimes.

Step 2

Ask pupils to brainstorm in pairs how they know when they are working hard.

Step 3

In a class plenary session, write pupils' views on the board. A sample of pupils from Years 7 to 11 in a Nottinghamshire comprehensive school came up with the following list.

> - The sets we are in
> - The marks, grades and merits we receive
> - Teachers' comments
> - Meeting deadlines
> - Self-assessment – sticking at things, doing our best

Teachers in the same school were asked how they recognised hard work in their lessons. They identified the following features.

> - *On-task behaviour* – pupils were fully engaged in the task in hand for most of the time
> - *Understanding* – pupils showed understanding in their interaction in class, through what they said and the questions they asked
> - *Outcomes* – pupils completed tasks with the quality of performance expected of them
> - *Pupils' enjoyment* – visible enjoyment, and through informal comments at the ends of lessons
> - *Pupils' body language* – the way they sat, and the hum of purposeful activity

Step 4

Invite pupil comment on both sets of features, and try to arrive at a common understanding. Such a consensus at the Nottinghamshire school might have produced the following.

> ## PUPILS IN THIS CLASS WORK HARD WHEN
>
> - They concentrate on a task, and stick at it
> - They ask questions to clarify their understanding
> - They finish work on time
> - They focus on quality

© John Beresford 2003 – *Creating the Conditions to Involve Pupils in Their Learning*

Activity 6.3: working hard at homework

Context

The ability to work hard when unsupervised is a key attribute of the lifelong learner. The completion of homework tasks represents one of the opportunities for pupils to develop this attribute. Teachers will be interested in the amount of homework that pupils do, as well as the home circumstances in which it is done. Questionnaire formats are provided in one of the other books in this series (Beresford 1998a: 53–8) that can be administered to gather this information. However, pupils are more likely to work hard at homework where they see the point of what is set.

Briefing

Aim

- To provide teachers with an activity to assess pupils' awareness of why homework is set.

Process

As with the other activities in this chapter, this exercise can be undertaken as a class activity. It should again be done at the beginning of a new phase of pupils' education, or when homework is first set in the school. There are four stages involved. Step 1 seeks to ascertain how many pupils enjoy homework (or in the case of pupils who have not formerly been set homework, how many enjoy doing schoolwork at home). Step 2 asks pupils why they think homework is set, and Step 3 lists pupils' views. Step 4 involves the presentation of teachers' opinions, and participants try to reconcile the views into a common understanding of the aims and purposes of homework.

Step 1

In a whole-class session, ask pupils how many of them like homework. If they are young pupils who have never been set formal homework, ask how many like doing schoolwork at home. From experience, the number of positive responses will be low, and you can share a joke about homework before moving on to its serious purposes.

Step 2

Having made the point that homework is set for various reasons, ask pupils in pairs to think about what those reasons might be.

Step 3

In a class plenary session, list pupils' responses on the board. Some Year 8 pupils in a Nottinghamshire school came up with the following reasons (presented in rank order).

- To develop independent learning skills
- To learn more
- To finish off tasks started in lessons
- For teachers to check pupils' understanding
- To enable pupils to review learning in school
- To do more work on a particular topic
- To improve pupil understanding
- To help with revision for exams
- For teachers to assess pupils' independent learning skills
- For pupils to assess their own understanding
- To prepare for future classwork
- Teacher revenge for pupils' bad behaviour
- There is no point

Step 4

Compare the list of pupils' perceived reasons with those listed, perhaps, in the school's homework policy. The group of Nottinghamshire Year 8 pupils had had discussions with their teachers about the purposes of homework, and the list of reasons provided to an external researcher bears testimony to the effectiveness of those discussions, and the extent to which pupils had absorbed the points in the policy. You might want to disassociate yourself from any vindictive feelings in setting homework!

You may also feel, as with Activity 6.2, that the consensus is worth reproducing graphically. A possible format is presented below.

© John Beresford 2003 – Creating the Conditions to Involve Pupils in Their Learning

WE DO HOMEWORK BECAUSE...

- It helps us learn to learn by ourselves
- It helps us learn more than we can in school
- It helps us to improve our understanding of what we do in school
- It helps us think about our work, and what we are learning
- It gives us a chance to finish work started in school
- It helps us to prepare for lessons, so that we can be fully involved in our learning
- It helps us to remember things, and in our revision
- It gives teachers clues and ideas about how to make us better learners

IT'S NOT A PUNISHMENT!!!!

Activity 6.4: acknowledging hard work

Context

Part of the way in which pupils know they are working hard is the response of the teachers for whom they are producing the work. Schools have rewards and sanctions systems and marking policies that go some way in determining the response of their teachers to the various levels of effort shown by their pupils. There are also a number of ways in which teachers informally provide signals to pupils about their views on the effort put into a piece of work.

Briefing

Aim

• To provide teachers with a schedule to assess pupil preferences of different kinds of 'reward' systems used in their schools.

Process

This schedule is part of the larger questionnaire from which the schedule for Activity 4.2 was also drawn. Teachers might want to combine the two, and administer them at the same time. As with the schedule in Activity 4.2, teachers can modify this one if they wish, in order to accommodate the practices in their own schools. The schedule again takes little time to fill in, and can be fitted in at the start of a registration or tutorial session. The activity involves three steps. In Step 1, the questionnaire is administered, in Step 2 the data are collated and Step 3, if necessary, involves the modification of classroom practices in the light of preferences expressed by pupils.

© John Beresford 2003 – Creating the Conditions to Involve Pupils in Their Learning

Step 1   The questionnaire takes about five minutes for pupils to fill in. You might want to amend some of the statements to reflect the systems within your school.

HOW DO YOU LIKE HARD WORK TO BE REWARDED?

The teachers in the school are interested in which kinds of reward for hard work you respond to best. Please fill in the following questionnaire. **We do not need to know your name.**

_____

I AM IN CLASS _____   I AM A   BOY   GIRL

(please circle the correct answer)

Please circle which of the four words after each of the following statements best reflects your feelings.

I prefer this type of reward for good work:

(a) Praise from the teacher	RARELY	SOMETIMES	OFTEN	ALWAYS
(b) A written comment in my book	RARELY	SOMETIMES	OFTEN	ALWAYS
(c) Merits/stickers	RARELY	SOMETIMES	OFTEN	ALWAYS
(d) A certificate	RARELY	SOMETIMES	OFTEN	ALWAYS
(e) Sweets	RARELY	SOMETIMES	OFTEN	ALWAYS
(f) A letter home to my parents	RARELY	SOMETIMES	OFTEN	ALWAYS
(g) Good comments in Comments Book	RARELY	SOMETIMES	OFTEN	ALWAYS

Thank you for filling in this questionnaire.

Step 2

You now need to collate the data. By scoring 'Rarely' responses for each statement as 1, 'Sometimes' as 2, 'Often' 3 and 'Always' 4, and then working out the average score for each statement for each gender-group in each year-group to whom you have administered the questionnaire, you can get an at-a-glance assessment of the comparative weightings of each of the seven factors listed. Scores above 3.0 indicate high preference levels. Below are data collected from the Essex school that used the schedule.

I prefer this type of reward for good work:	Average scores for each statement			
	Year 7 boys	Year 7 girls	Year 8 boys	Year 8 girls
Praise from the teacher	2.4	2.5	2.5	2.7
A written comment in my book	2.8	2.7	2.7	2.7
Merits/stickers	3.4	3.4	3.3	3.3
A certificate	3.0	3.1	3.2	3.1
Sweets	2.9	2.8	2.5	2.4
A letter home to my parents	2.5	2.3	2.6	2.1
Good comments in Comments Book	2.7	3.4	3.2	3.0

Four of the rewards listed received favourable ratings (above 2.5) from all four groups. Pupils showed some preference for the more public and considered manifestations of teacher approval – merits and stickers, certificates and (with the more lukewarm response of Year 7 boys) comments reported in a ledger on public display in the school's reception area.

Step 3

You will now want to review your practice in the light of the data you have collated. Using the listed headings above, the following questions may help.

- Should the praise I give to pupils be in front of the class, or in private?
- When I write comments at the end of a piece of work, should the praise come first or last?
- Am I clear on the criteria I use to give stickers, merits and certificates?
- Are there any other ways my pupils would like to be rewarded?

© *John Beresford 2003 – Creating the Conditions to Involve Pupils in Their Learning*

CHAPTER 7

Adjustment to school

We have suggested in the previous chapters a range of strategies that teachers can use to impact upon pupil behaviour and, in so doing, improve the quality of pupil learning. We believe that the provision of a set of parameters within which pupils can conduct their daily life in school is also important: 'If we hope pupils will value and enjoy learning, we need to be able to create a learning environment in which pupils will feel secure and valued' (Hopkins *et al.* 1997: 31).

Clearly an important pre-condition of improving learning at school is ensuring that pupils like school sufficiently to attend regularly: 'If a segment of the school population is not present physically or is feeling alienated or absent mentally, of what value is excellent pedagogy?' (Testerman 1996). Although English pupils are apparently less positive about schooling than Russian pupils (Elliott *et al.* 1997) and French pupils (Osborn 1997a; 1997b), it is our experience that the majority of pupils in all schools like coming to school. It is also our experience that the main reason stated for liking school, particularly after the first year of secondary education, is that it is a place where pupils can meet their friends. Reasons for not liking school focus primarily upon specific teachers and specific subjects. Complaints about school rules are often made in Years 8 to 10, where we have noted that pupils' senses of justice and equity are most marked. Hence complaints are directed less, for example, against the imposition of a dress code than against teachers' lack of consistency in enforcing it. In schools with sixth forms on site, and where a different dress code applies, a number of complaints arise about consistency from pupils lower down the school. Some pupils question why teachers are not subject to the same behaviour restrictions, for example over smoking on the school premises, as pupils.

We have found that, where teachers are prepared to negotiate with their pupils about the rules within which both operate, that 'pupils will be self-controlling within the set boundaries' (Hopkins *et al.* 1997: 32). Compliance to school rules in IQEA schools, as elsewhere (see, for example, Hord 1997), is seen as a key component of success at school. When we have questioned pupils (mainly boys) who are deemed disruptive in class by their teachers, they have justified their disruptive behaviour by claiming that lessons were boring, or that they did not understand the work they had been asked to do. They had few complaints about school rules or codes of classroom conduct, although they freely admitted they had broken them. Our observations of on-task and off-task behaviour in a range of lessons across a range of schools suggest that boys' off-task behaviour is often more explosive than girls', but we would agree from talking to pupils that 'schools must not assume that the majority of pupils whose behaviour is compliant are actually satisfied with their experiences at school' (Campbell 1993). We have a number of well-documented instances of so-called disruptive pupils being more on-task than the 'control' pupil we have also been asked to observe.

We would agree with others that disruptive behaviour should not necessarily be regarded as a function of social deviancy or as an indicator of special educational needs (Elliott 1997), and that work with peer groups rather than individuals to secure engagement with learning is often more appropriate (Hickey and Fitzclarence 1999). Setting targets related to behaviour has provided one arena for such negotiation to take place, even with very young children (Castelijns 1996). We have also encouraged schools to negotiate contracts with teaching groups, whereby, in return for certain behaviours by pupils in class, teachers will themselves guarantee certain behaviours, for example well-planned lessons and prompt feedback on work done.

Pupils appear to be more comfortable with their working environment

- when their teachers are seen to be just (Activity 7.1);
- when pupils can accept the sense of having school rules (Activity 7.2);
- where pupils attend school regularly (Activity 7.3);
- when pupils conform to the rules that regulate the school community (Activity 7.4).

Activity 7.1: making rules in the classroom

Context

Pupils' adherence to codes of conduct that regulate the environment in which they learn is an essential element in the development of learning autonomy. Without such adherence, lessons become disrupted, and it is difficult for learning to take place because teachers become preoccupied with keeping order. In most classrooms such codes of conduct are formulated by teachers and, while they are invariably based upon commonsense principles to facilitate pupil learning, our experience is that some pupils feel no sense of ownership of them because they have had no input into their formulation. Where there is no consensus on the underlying principles of the codes of conduct, some pupils might feel that elements are unjust and inequitable. Where this is the case, pupils might feel some justification in disrupting lessons.

Briefing

Aim

- To provide teachers with a strategy to devise a code of classroom conduct which accommodates the views of pupils.

Process

This activity is again of sufficient importance for the learning of pupils to be undertaken early on in a new phase of their learning, perhaps when they are starting in a new school or in a new class. It is structured in six steps and can be done in a whole-class session, perhaps spreading into a second lesson. Step 1 involves asking pupils to think about the qualities of a good pupil. This can be done as a paired or group activity. In Step 2, teachers list the views reported in a plenary class session and then, in Step 3, groups or pairs of pupils are asked to suggest a few rules relating to classroom behaviour which can enable them to be good pupils. In Step 4, the suggestions from the pupils are collected, and Step 5 seeks to come to some consensus on six or so rules that the class as a whole would be happy to follow. In Step 6, the teacher offers the class certain teaching behaviours in return. This indicates to the class that they are devising a code that extends to all members of the learning community and that the code is a contract based upon mutual respect. It also highlights the sense of justice and equity in the arrangements.

© John Beresford 2003 – Creating the Conditions to Involve Pupils in Their Learning

Step 1   Ask pupils to brainstorm the qualities of a good pupil. This can be done in pairs or in groups.

Step 2   In a whole-class session, list pupils' responses on the board. Highlight the most common responses. A group of pupils from Years 7 to 9 in a Leicester comprehensive school produced the following list. The responses are in rank order.

> A good pupil:
>
> - is well-behaved
> - listens
> - works hard/does his or her best
> - wants to learn
> - respects self and others
> - stays on-task
> - obeys teachers
> - works quietly
> - is friendly/polite

Step 3   With such a list on the board, ask pupils (again in groups or pairs) to devise about half a dozen rules to allow for such behaviours.

Step 4   Collect suggestions from the pupils in a whole-class plenary session, and write them on the board.

Step 5   Come to some class consensus on the rules that best allow for the behaviours like those listed in Step 2. Using the Leicester example, such a list might look like the one below.

> - We do nothing that disrupts the learning of others.
> - We listen when someone is addressing the whole class, or when someone is talking to us in a pair or a group.
> - Where the teacher has to give instructions, we obey them.
> - We concentrate on the tasks we have been given.
> - We work as quietly as we can.
> - We treat other people in the classroom with politeness and respect.

   © John Beresford 2003 – Creating the Conditions to Involve Pupils in Their Learning

Step 6

You now offer to pupils what you will do as part of the code of conduct. This does not need to be anything extra to what you would do as a class teacher, but the gesture emphasises the contractual nature of the code of conduct – that it is intended to embrace all members of the classroom community and that the arrangements have an underlying fairness and equity. You would be advised to produce, or get pupils to produce, an *aide-mémoire* of the exercise. It might look like this:

LEARNING IS THE MOST IMPORTANT ACTIVITY THAT TAKES PLACE IN THIS CLASSROOM

To help learning to take place, pupils have agreed to

- Do nothing that disrupts the learning of others
- Listen when someone is talking to them
- Obey teachers when they have to give instructions
- Concentrate on the tasks they've been given
- Work as quietly as they can
- Treat other people in the classroom with politeness and respect

To help learning to take place, the teacher has agreed to

- Turn up to lessons fully prepared and on time
- Explain tasks and give instructions clearly
- Keep order according to the agreed code of conduct

Activity 7.2: seeing the point of school rules

Context

Pupil adherence to the rules that regulate the larger community of the school is also important to learning. Pupils who frequently break school rules are liable to be suspended, and will miss important parts of their education. Some pupils' attitudes to school rules often determine their attitude to school and, just as those who have little affinity with their teachers often struggle, those who are unable to adjust to the conventions and rules of their particular school often find learning in the school a difficult process. As with codes of classroom conduct, such pupils may feel a greater sense of ownership of school rules if they have been able to have some input into their formulation. With the size of many secondary schools, this is a more difficult process to organise than contributing to rules regulating classroom behaviours.

Briefing

Aims

- To provide a strategy by which teachers can determine the views of pupils on the importance of adherence to school rules.
- To provide teachers with an opportunity to justify various school rules.

Process

There are two steps to this activity. In Step 1, teachers should ask pupils why an organisation the size of a school needs rules. They should then rehearse the school rules with the class. Step 2 asks pupils why they think specific school rules have been created. This provides an opportunity for teachers to justify each of the school rules and to indicate the process, if such exists, by which pupils can set about getting school rules changed. It also gives an opportunity to discuss various issues relating to the school as an organisation.

Step 1

Ask pupils why large organisations need rules, and why schools in particular need rules. Brainstorming can be done by pupils in pairs or in groups. List their suggestions on the board in a plenary session.

A group of Year 10 pupils, deemed by the staff of a north Nottinghamshire comprehensive to be disruptive and 'anti-school', gave the following reasons for the importance of school rules.

School rules:

- Are necessary to retain order
- Provide a decent working environment
- Teach self-control and respect for others
- Impose conformity
- Deprive pupils of right of personal expression

Now remind pupils of the school rules.

Step 2

In the light of what pupils have said during the plenary session at the end of Step 1, ask pupils to discuss in their pairs or groups why they think each of the school rules has been created. Challenge the more negative comments ('Is it likely that this school wants its pupils to conform unquestioningly?', 'Why should teachers want to impose limits on personal expression?').

Where school rules clearly fulfil the purposes identified by pupils, there will be little questioning about why they were created. Where school rules do not appear to have any of the identified purposes, it can give rise to an interesting discussion around the school as an organisation. The following questions might be posed by pupils.

- Should school rules be school community rules? (Should they also apply to teachers?)
- To what extent should the behaviour of post-16 pupils be regulated, or should school community rules also apply to them?
- Whose school is it anyway? (What external agencies should schools take cognisance of when formulating their rules?)

Where your school has procedures in place for pupils to have an input into making and changing school rules, the discussion should end with you pointing out the process that students can follow.

Activity 7.3: making pupils want to attend school

Context

Attendance at school is fundamental to developing the learning capacity of pupils. Without it, pupils are unlikely to have the opportunity to develop the key learning skills and acquire the necessary knowledge to become lifelong learners. It is because of the debilitating effects of truancy upon pupil learning that successive governments have laid such stress upon good school attendance, and that schools have made such efforts to raise and maintain pupil attendance rates. The reasons why pupils truant are multiple and complex, but schools will find it useful to know what habitual truants like and dislike about school, in order to devise individual or group programmes to encourage school attendance.

Briefing

Aim

- To provide schools with a strategy for determining what pupils like and dislike about school, as the basis of programmes to raise and maintain levels of attendance.

Process

For schools with only a handful of habitual truants, the strategy might best be followed with individual pupils. In schools where truancy is a more widespread problem, it might be appropriate to undertake the activity with whole classes, early on in the school year. There are four steps involved. Step 1 asks pupils to jot down (anonymously) what they like about school, and what they do not like. In Step 2, teachers collate the data, and present the findings to the individual or class. Step 3 allows pupils to discuss whether any of the reasons for not liking school ever outweigh the reasons for liking it, and whether in any of these circumstances staying away from school is justified. Step 4 involves a plenary discussion, where broader issues about the function of education may be considered.

© John Beresford 2003 – *Creating the Conditions to Involve Pupils in Their Learning*

Step 1   Ask the pupils to jot down on a sheet of paper what they like about school. Stress that you do not need to know pupils' names. Collect in the sheets. On another sheet, ask them to jot down what they *don't* like about school. Again stress that contributions should be anonymous.

Step 2   Collate the results. Clearly this will take some time if the activity is done with the whole class. Tell the class you will be presenting the results in a forth-coming lesson.

　　　Below is a table of results from the responses of 100 pupils in Years 7 to 9 of a Nottingham comprehensive school. The numbers indicate the rank order.

Features liked	Year 7	Year 8	Year 9
Meeting/working with friends	1	1	1
Specific subjects	2	2	2
A fun element in some lessons	3	–	–
Friendly/pleasant teachers	4	–	–
Breaktimes	7=	3=	3=
Lunch-time	7=	3=	3=
Some lessons	5	3=	–
Element of activity in lessons	–	–	3=
Fridays	6	–	–
Some teachers	–	–	3=

Meeting and working with friends far outranked all other responses in Years 8 and 9.

Features disliked	Year 7	Year 8	Year 9
(Too much) homework	2	1	3=
Some teachers	4	3=	2
Specific subjects	1	3=	8=
Limited freedom at lunch-time	–	–	1
Some lessons	5=	2	8=
Litter	3	–	8=
Some pupils	8=	3=	8=
Dress code	–	3=	5=
One-way system	–	–	3=
Specific teachers	8=	–	5=
Afternoon break too short	8=	7	–
Early start to school day	5=	–	–
Some topics hard	–	–	5=
Pupils disrupting lessons	5=	–	–

Homework far outranked all other responses in Year 8.

Step 3

Present the findings to pupils in a visual form. Ask them to discuss in pairs or groups whether any of the reasons outlined in 'Dislikes' outweigh any of the 'Likes', and if they do whether they are ever a sufficient reason to stay away from school. Quite reasonably, those citing 'other pupils' as one of their dislikes might argue that bullying that is not being addressed by the school is sufficient reason. This provides an opportunity for you to explain the procedures in the school for dealing with specific issues, like bullying. Procedures relating to pupils having an input into how the school is run, for example by representation through a school council, can also be discussed. You might want to widen the area of discussion to talk about the importance of education (and of attending school) in terms of future career, work and citizenship demands.

© John Beresford 2003 – Creating the Conditions to Involve Pupils in Their Learning

Activity 7.4: adhering to school and classroom rules

Context

Pupils who do not adhere to codes of classroom conduct or to school rules, be they drawn up by teachers or negotiated with the pupils themselves, harm their own learning as well as that of their peers. Misbehaviour often disrupts teaching, leads to the punishment of the pupils involved, including their exclusion from the classroom or school, and may affect in a negative way their attitudes to the school and to the teachers who work there. Those pupils who routinely misbehave often become isolated from the main body of pupils, and their views about learning are discounted. However, as well as being part of a rehabilitation process, listening to what these pupils have to say about learning can also provide interesting insights into teaching and learning in schools.

Briefing

Aim

- To provide teachers with an interview schedule to explore with disruptive pupils why they misbehave.

Process

This schedule needs to be administered by someone not known to the pupils. Pupils who have been selected for interview because they are labelled as disruptive are unlikely to provide authentic responses to what are sensitive questions if they are asked by someone who is aware of their reputation and of incidents that have contributed to it. In the two schools in Cambridgeshire and Nottinghamshire where the interviews were conducted, an external researcher was used.

The activity comprises three steps, the first of which involves organising and holding the interviews. Pupils need not be told that they have been chosen because they are disruptive, merely that the school is interested in their views on aspects of classroom behaviour. The interviewer must be chosen with care. He or she should not know the pupils, and preferably should not be given their names, so that anonymity is guaranteed. Step 2 involves the collation of the results. Ideally this should be done by the interviewer, although teachers can use the interviewer's field notes. In Step 3, the results are fed back to those interviewed and the findings are discussed with the pupils.

Step 1   Adapt the interview schedule to your own requirements. Identify the pupils you wish to be interviewed and choose someone to interview them. It needs to be a person who is not known to the students, and who does not know them. The pupils should not be told that they are being interviewed because they have been identified as disruptive, but because they will have interesting things to say about classroom behaviour. Hold the interviews.

Step 2   If you have been fortunate enough to obtain the services of a professional interviewer, he or she may be prepared to write you a report. Otherwise you can collate your own findings, using the interviewer's field notes.

Step 3   Feed back and discuss the findings with the pupils who have been interviewed. From the Cambridgeshire and Nottinghamshire interviews, three kinds of disruptive pupil were identified. A small group disrupted alone, and internalised the causes as being part of their personality. An equally small group externalised the causes, blaming others and claiming to be disruptive in reaction to those around them. The third group, by far the largest, contextualised their disruption, misbehaving, for example, when they disliked a particular teaching approach. If such categories emerge from your findings, discuss them with the pupils. Again, you might want to widen the discussion around the importance of education, and any alternative ways (other than classroom disruption) available in the school of providing feedback on teaching and learning.

INTERVIEW SCHEDULE ON CLASSROOM BEHAVIOUR

1. Do you ever misbehave in class?
    Why?

2. What do you think causes lessons to be disrupted?

3. What kind of pupils cause disruption?

4. What should a teacher do about classroom disruption?

5. What shouldn't a teacher do?

6. Which classroom rules do you remember?

7. How do you feel about the rules of classroom conduct?

    © John Beresford 2003 – Creating the Conditions to Involve Pupils in Their Learning

CHAPTER 8

Changing the culture of the classroom and the school

Involving the pupil voice

Within IQEA, it has been a basic premise that the administration of the various surveys carries with it some responsibility, if the whole process is not to be dismissed as a complete waste of time by those being consulted:

> The mapping techniques entail an imperative which requires, not just a response, but a particular kind of response. The questioners are bound by the authenticity of their authority not just to listen, but to listen with care and respect and to reply in ways which acknowledge and demonstrate the legitimacy of standpoints other than their own.　　　(Fielding 1995)

It remains a point of concern within the IQEA project that, although the school project coordinators routinely feed back the results of the Management and Classroom (Teacher) Conditions Surveys to staff, schools do not feed back the results of the Pupil Conditions Survey to pupils. While a large number of schools do not have the appropriate forum in which to feed back and discuss such results, for example a pupil council, many increasingly do. We believe that the main reason for such reticence is that the planning of teaching experiences in the classroom is still regarded as the exclusive concern of teachers. One of the main lessons to be drawn from this book is that it is not.

Using the work of Thiessen (1997; 1998) and Fielding (2001), it is possible to build a continuum of teacher responses to researching the pupil voice. This continuum is presented in Figure 8.1. At one extreme, there is no research undertaken that involves canvassing the views of pupils. While teachers may feel some responsibility in developing the learning repertoire of their pupils, they regard the delivery of the curriculum as solely their own responsibility. Pupils are passive absorbers of received knowledge, and feel they have no voice in the school.

Further along the continuum, pupils are regarded as data sources. Research is organised by staff on issues primarily of interest to staff, and the findings of the research are rarely fed back to the pupils themselves. The findings may be acted upon by staff, or they may not be. Teaching and learning are still very much in the control of the teachers. Many of the schools within the IQEA project fall into this category.

Even further along, and at some distance from the previous category in terms of attitudes towards pupils, are schools that undertake research using pupils, but that feed back the results in order to initiate a debate with the pupil body on the findings and issues raised. The research agenda is still very much dictated by the teachers, but there is some acknowledgement that pupils have a contribution to make to the improvement of teaching and learning in the school beyond responding to surveys. What these schools are prepared to do is to seek amplification of responses given in the Pupil Conditions Survey, in order to inform further their planning processes.

A fourth category sees schools where teachers and pupils co-research teaching and learning issues. As in the case of an American west coast research collaborative involving both groups, the focus of research is generally selected by the teachers (Blum 1997; Shaughnessy and Kushman 1997). Where pupils interview each other, research is more likely to present 'their authentic voice' and less likely 'to be refracting their meanings through the lens of [teachers'] own interests and concerns' (Rudduck *et al.* 1996a, quoted in Cooper and Fielding 1998).

At the end of the continuum are the schools where the subject of school research is 'in the collective control of the pupils themselves' (Fielding 2001). Pupils research their own areas of concern, while teachers in the school research theirs. The co-research process described in the fourth category also takes place, though the teachers and pupils in schools that fit into this final category work in teams on topics chosen by the pupils as well as by the teachers. One such school within the IQEA network has set up a *Pupils as Researchers* project (Jackson *et al.* 1998; Fielding 2001), and one or two others are following its example. In one of these schools, pupils feed back to staff, senior management and at governors' meetings and have given presentations at national and international research conferences. The school holds it own annual Pupil Voice Conference, which attracted 300 pupil delegates in 2000 (Jackson *et al.* 1998).

These five stations – along what I have called the continuum of pupil involvement in school-based research – in effect describe five distinctive sets of teacher attitudes to the role of pupils in school improvement. They also suggest five discrete cultures, defined in terms of the extent of pupil participation in the design of their teaching and learning experiences. In that respect they provide useful indicators to all those involved in the process of school improvement – be they teachers, pupils or external consultants – of the various stages of pupil involvement in school improvement.

The fourth and fifth stations described above owe as much to following principles of democratic involvement in the running of schools as they do to skilling pupils as learners. The sets of attitudes described in each send out the strongest possible message that pupils' views are integral to the effective running of schools. They acknowledge the importance of a harmonious and focused pupil community as a factor in school improvement (see Hargreaves 2001). But the systems they describe are time-consuming, may take pupils out of the classroom and require a great deal of organisation. As the consultant to the *Pupils as Researchers* project – mentioned in the fifth category – concedes, teachers researching and presenting the pupil voice may be the only option available for most schools (Cooper and Fielding 1998). From the standpoint of this chapter, a shift to station three would represent a massive sea change for most schools in their regard for pupils' views.

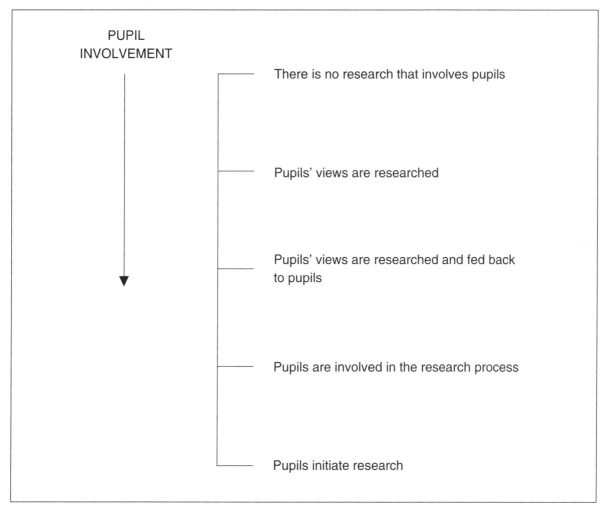

PUPIL
INVOLVEMENT

There is no research that involves pupils

Pupils' views are researched

Pupils' views are researched and fed back
to pupils

Pupils are involved in the research process

Pupils initiate research

Figure 8.1 A continuum of pupil involvement in their learning

Changing the culture of the classroom and the school

This book has constructed an instrument that can be used to assess pupils' views on the classroom conditions necessary for school improvement to take place. In so doing, it has been necessary to reconceptualise the classroom conditions described elsewhere (for example, in Hopkins *et al.* 1997) so that they are recognisable to pupils. These original conditions relate to a culture of teacher collaboration and enquiry into effective teaching and learning. Inasmuch as they constitute teacher behaviours, they are grounded firmly within the teacher community. In effect, they help to describe the culture relating to teacher activity in the school and classroom.

What have been described in the book as the pupil conditions present a set of behaviours firmly grounded within the pupil community. The complementary nature of many of these behaviours when compared with the corresponding list of teacher behaviours is unsurprising, given that both teachers and pupils engage in the classroom in the processes of teaching and learning. What this book has argued is that, just as schools can develop their own management capacity and their staff's teaching capacity for school improvement, it is also possible to develop pupils' learning capacity so that more effective learning can take place. In this chapter the culture needed to sustain this development both in the school and in the classroom is outlined.

Because of the changes in communications technology and workplace practices described earlier in this book, there are different expectations placed on pupils when they emerge from the period of compulsory schooling. They are expected to be numerate, literate and to have a basic general knowledge related to the society in which they live. The sustained improvement in public examination results throughout the 1990s and into the new century suggests that the English educational system is comparatively proficient in equipping pupils to meet these expectations. Pupils are also expected to be adaptable to change, to be able to work effectively in teams, to be multi-skilled, to want to learn and to know how to learn. A great deal of educational research, including the body that relates to this book, suggests that the system is less successful in these areas.

These shifting expectations require a change, or rather an adjustment, of role for teachers. As well as communicating a discrete body of knowledge, teachers need to teach pupils how to learn. Such a change of role requires variation in the nature of classroom activity, but more importantly it requires a change in the way teachers regard pupils, and subsequently in the way pupils regard themselves. In essence it requires a change in the culture of the classroom and the school.

Schools currently have a statutory obligation to deliver the National Curriculum, they are inspected on their ability to deliver that curriculum, their pupils are regularly tested on their knowledge of it. This systems model has largely concentrated on inputs and outputs, and has generally ignored the internal processes involved. It might be argued that government has appeared to be more concerned with the short-term results that the system can achieve than with the ways in which they have been achieved. This book has suggested that a focus on process is important in the development of autonomous, multi-skilled and motivated learners, whom society and the workplace require now and in the future. The Advanced Skills and Key Stage 3 Strategies are belated acknowledgements by the government that teaching about the processes of learning is at least as important as what is learnt.

This required shift from an exclusive preoccupation with the delivery of the National Curriculum to learning about how to learn requires a change in the culture of the school and of the classroom. Education needs to become a joint venture of teacher and pupil to find ever more effective ways of learning, ways that expand pupils' learning repertoire while at the same time meeting pupils' individual learning needs and styles. It needs to become a joint venture that seeks to harness new technology, new knowledge and the new ways of communicating knowledge, to pupil learning. Education must become something done *with* pupils rather than *to* them.

It is a joint venture because it requires, as suggested earlier in this chapter, an ongoing dialogue about teaching and learning between teachers and pupils. The dialogue is ongoing as teachers accommodate new knowledge and fresh approaches to teaching and learning within their own repertoire, and try these new models with their pupils. It requires teachers and pupils to develop a language of teaching and learning to enable such a dialogue to take place, and it requires teachers to instruct pupils in various learning methods. Pupils need to be able to develop their own understanding and meaning in relation to what and how they are taught, and to become empowered in the sense that they can draw upon this understanding to pursue their own learning. They start to become autonomous learners. As the awareness of pupils in these fields grows, teachers are able to evaluate with them the various strategies being used to facilitate their learning. Pupils become critical and reflective learners, but with a criticism born of knowledge and self-knowledge rather than malice.

It is but a short step to give pupils some say in the circumstances in which they learn, and to involve them in formulating the codes of conduct that regulate the learning process. Rules systems need to become the subject of negotiation rather than imposition. Taking heed of pupil views involves teachers in giving space and paying attention to dissident voices, and respecting difference. Where such differences are aired, pupils have less cause to complain about the injustices and inequities of systems to which they have been able to contribute, for example in the formulation of codes of classroom conduct. Such codes are less likely to be transgressed where they have been the subject of discussion and justification involving both pupils and teachers. Concurring with the views of another writer on pupils' control of their own learning, it is clear that such 'Democratic participation in school . . . presents an immense challenge, not only to teachers' own sense of professionalism but also with and for the pupils themselves' (Crozier 1999).

Pupils need to move from being passive absorbers of received knowledge to a group actively involved in, and taking some responsibility for, its own education. An ongoing and informed dialogue between teachers and pupils about learning and the circumstances in which that learning takes place is an overt symbol of respect for the authenticity of the pupil voice, but it is also a recognition of pupil investment in the conduct of their learning. That investment can be assumed to entail a commitment to negotiated codes of conduct relating to the processes of pupil learning. Where such a commitment exists, teachers and pupils can also negotiate sanctions for when such codes are transgressed, for example when homework is not done.

It is apparent from our own research that many pupils would welcome such types of active involvement. It is also apparent, from our limited experience in IQEA schools of such active involvement of pupils in their own learning, that teachers have nothing to fear from the comments on teaching of a well-informed pupil body. In such circumstances, comments have been insightful about pedagogy, as well as accepting of the need for some regulation in the conduct of teaching and learning (see Beresford 1999c; Stokes 1999).

In such a culture, teachers facilitate their pupils' 'progression in responsibility and autonomy' (Rudduck 1998). They contextualise work, they explain and routinely justify methods of teaching and learning in the classroom, they become apologists for the National Curriculum, they discuss success criteria with pupils and they take part in a joint evaluation of their own work, as well as that of their pupils. In such a classroom, 'imposed change through the authority of the teacher' is replaced by an exploration of 'the need for change with the pupils themselves' (Rudduck and Flutter 2000). Teachers continue to explore with their colleagues innovative ways of teaching, present these to pupils while coaching them in the necessary skills required to take full advantage of them, and feed back their own and their pupils' evaluation of them as teaching and learning techniques. Hence the activity associated with the culture of the teacher community in an improving school will enrich and sustain the learning culture of the pupil community.

The contention of this chapter, and indeed of the whole book, echoes the sentiment of a veteran school improver elsewhere: 'Change will not occur unless there is an alteration of power relationships among those in the system and within the classroom' (Sarason 1990: xiv). The power relationship relates to a necessary change of regard by teachers towards their pupils. The needs of current and future society for citizens and workers who are adaptable, multi-skilled, and able and willing to access sources of knowledge, can best be met by fundamental changes in the way that pupils are educated. Some of these changes are currently being introduced. But they also require a concomitant change in the way teachers and pupils interact. Teaching has to embrace 'much more openness and reciprocity' (Fielding 2001), and pupils have to take a shared responsibility for the success of teaching and learning in the classroom. Our own research within IQEA, as well as research elsewhere (Barsby 1991; Connolly 1997; Thiessen 1997), suggests that this process can start before secondary education, and indeed as early as Key Stage 1. As school improvers, we need to focus our efforts upon the empowerment of pupils. We need to help schools move from station to station along the continuum of pupil involvement. The journey through the educational system needs to be one of increasing autonomy and learning independence for the pupil. As teachers help pupils in this journey, they learn new ways of teaching and learning which feed into the pupils' growth process. Education becomes a joint venture where teachers and their pupils grow together.

APPENDIX

Administering the Pupil Conditions Surveys: secondary and primary versions

Using the Pupil Conditions Rating Scale

The Pupil Conditions Surveys in this Appendix can be administered at any time in order to gauge pupils' feelings about their experiences at school. Many IQEA schools administer them at the start of their involvement in a school improvement initiative, in order to help identify areas or issues that may need addressing. They sometimes also administer them at the end of an initiative, in order to see whether pupils' attitudes have changed.

The Conditions Surveys are best administered in classroom sessions. Pupils are required to tick whether certain behaviours in the school occur rarely, sometimes, often or nearly always. Where a number of pupils have reading difficulties it might be appropriate for the teacher to read out each of the statements to the class. This is a strategy often favoured by the teachers of very young pupils (the survey has been administered to Reception-aged children, but we would advise that it is more appropriate for use with Year 2 pupils and above). We suggest 25 per cent samples of particular year-groups for secondary schools (tutorial/registration groups are useful because they tend to be of mixed ability).

The data are presented as Likert scores. This involves scoring each 'rarely' response as 1, 'sometimes' as 2, 'often' as 3 and 'nearly always' as 4. This new total is then divided by the number of respondents to each statement, in order to find an average score. Average scores of between 1.0 and 2.0 suggest that behaviours occur comparatively rarely, scores of 2.1 to 2.9 that they occur occasionally, and scores of over 3 that they occur almost as a matter of course. The table format provided is intended to enable schools to note at a glance differences in response to individual statements by different genders and year-groups.

The Pupil Conditions Surveys have been administered in over 80 secondary and primary schools across the country, involving some 11,000 students. The data in Tables 1 and 2 are reproduced in order to provide a comparison if you choose to administer either of the surveys yourself.

General findings   There are certain general themes that emerge from the collated data. The sample of primary pupils outside Years 5 and 6 is still quite low, so generalisations relating to specific year-groups should be regarded as tentative.

- Pupils of both genders in both primary and secondary schools highlight the high frequency of behaviours over which they feel they have some control, for example school attendance, good behaviour and finding classroom equipment.
- Girls are generally more contented at school than boys. They almost consistently rate the frequency of each behaviour higher than boys in the same year-group.
- The low frequency of pupil reflection and seeking help from teachers means that, in the absence of these key components, pupils will find it difficult to assess with any accuracy how well they are doing, and how they can improve.
- Opportunities for independent learning are limited in many schools. The incidence of problem solving is higher in the primary sector. The incidence of groupwork in schools appears to decline after Year 2.
- Secondary pupils feel that many of their teachers use a restricted teaching repertoire, and consequently they find many lessons uninteresting.
- Despite this, secondary pupils (like primary ones) generally show positive attitudes to work and behaving well.
- Of all primary-aged pupils, Year 5 boys are the most lukewarm about school: they like lessons less, and claim to work less hard, than any other group.
- Year 7 pupils are generally enthusiastic about their schools. They take greatest care about what they report to parents and are best able to access classroom equipment. As well as finding teachers more helpful than other year-groups, they are extremely enthusiastic about their lessons, claim to work harder than other years and are happier with school rules.
- Year 8 boys are discontented with their lot at school. They are the group least able to self-assess, the group with poorest relationships with teachers and the group whose self-perception of their behaviour is poorest.
- Of the girls, Year 10 are the most discontented. They are the least reflective of their gender, and are the least likely to use books for independent research, they have the poorest relationships with their teachers, they enjoy lessons the least and they have most complaints about school rules. Boys show similar traits in Year 11, which may have some impact upon their performance at GCSE.

A more detailed analysis of the secondary school data is available in Beresford (2003, in press).

Table 1 Pupils' average ratings of conditions in secondary schools, 1999–2002

		Y7 Boys	Y7 Girls	Y7 All	Y8 Boys	Y8 Girls	Y8 All	Y9 Boys	Y9 Girls	Y9 All	Y10 Boys	Y10 Girls	Y10 All	Y11 Boys	Y11 Girls	Y11 All	Y12 Boys	Y12 Girls	Y12 All	Y13 Boys	Y13 Girls	Y13 All
		705	788	1519	777	858	1642	1047	1034	2110	798	860	1687	721	748	1504	366	333	710	193	260	464
Self-assessment	1.1	2.2	2.2	2.2	1.9	2.0	1.9	1.9	1.9	1.9	1.8	1.8	1.8	1.9	1.9	1.9	2.1	2.2	2.2	2.2	2.2	2.2
	1.2	2.6	2.7	2.7	2.5	2.6	2.6	2.6	2.5	2.6	2.6	2.5	2.6	2.6	2.7	2.6	2.9	2.7	2.8	3.0	2.9	2.9
	1.3	3.0	3.1	3.1	3.0	3.1	3.0	2.8	2.8	2.8	2.7	2.8	2.7	2.6	2.9	2.7	2.7	2.8	2.8	2.4	2.6	2.5
	1.4	1.8	1.9	1.9	1.8	1.8	1.8	1.8	1.8	1.8	1.9	1.9	1.9	2.1	2.2	2.2	2.1	2.3	2.2	2.2	2.3	2.2
Independent learning	2.1	3.3	3.4	3.4	3.2	3.2	3.2	3.1	3.1	3.1	3.1	3.1	3.1	3.1	3.2	3.1	3.1	3.2	3.2	3.0	3.1	3.1
	2.2	2.4	2.5	2.5	2.3	2.3	2.3	2.3	2.2	2.2	2.3	2.2	2.2	2.3	2.3	2.3	2.4	2.2	2.3	2.4	2.2	2.3
	2.3	2.5	2.6	2.6	2.3	2.5	2.4	2.4	2.5	2.4	2.2	2.4	2.3	2.2	2.4	2.3	2.5	2.7	2.6	2.4	2.6	2.5
	2.4	2.3	2.7	2.5	2.2	2.5	2.4	2.3	2.5	2.4	2.0	2.3	2.2	2.0	2.4	2.2	2.6	3.0	2.8	2.6	3.0	2.8
Affinity to teachers	3.1	2.9	3.3	3.1	2.6	2.8	2.7	2.6	2.8	2.7	2.6	2.7	2.6	2.7	2.9	2.8	3.1	3.4	3.3	3.2	3.3	3.3
	3.2	2.8	2.9	2.8	2.6	2.6	2.6	2.5	2.5	2.5	2.4	2.4	2.4	2.3	2.4	2.4	2.6	2.7	2.7	2.6	2.6	2.6
	3.3	3.1	3.2	3.1	2.7	2.9	2.8	2.6	2.7	2.7	2.6	2.5	2.6	2.5	2.6	2.6	2.9	3.0	2.9	3.0	3.0	3.0
	3.4	2.4	2.7	2.6	2.4	2.5	2.4	2.3	2.3	2.3	2.2	2.3	2.2	2.3	2.5	2.4	2.7	2.7	2.7	2.7	2.8	2.8
Learning repertoire	4.1	2.4	2.4	2.4	2.2	2.2	2.2	2.2	2.2	2.2	2.1	2.0	2.1	2.2	2.1	2.1	1.9	1.9	1.9	2.1	2.0	2.0
	4.2	2.9	3.0	2.9	2.7	2.9	2.8	2.7	2.7	2.7	2.7	2.7	2.7	2.7	2.8	2.8	2.9	2.9	2.9	2.9	2.9	2.9
	4.3	2.5	2.5	2.5	2.1	2.2	2.1	2.1	2.1	2.1	2.0	2.0	2.0	2.0	2.1	2.0	2.3	2.5	2.4	2.3	2.5	2.4
	4.4	2.6	2.7	2.7	2.3	2.5	2.4	2.3	2.3	2.3	2.0	2.1	2.1	2.0	2.1	2.1	2.2	2.3	2.3	2.0	2.2	2.1
Orientation to learning	5.1	2.2	2.4	2.3	1.9	2.0	1.9	1.9	1.9	1.9	1.9	1.9	1.9	1.8	1.9	1.9	2.1	2.2	2.1	2.0	2.1	2.1
	5.2	3.1	3.3	3.2	2.8	3.1	3.0	2.9	3.0	2.9	2.7	3.0	2.8	2.7	2.9	2.8	2.9	3.1	3.0	2.6	3.0	2.8
	5.3	3.0	3.3	3.1	2.6	2.9	2.8	2.6	2.8	2.7	2.5	2.8	2.6	2.3	2.7	2.5	2.6	2.9	2.7	2.4	2.8	2.7
	5.4	3.0	3.2	3.1	2.7	2.8	2.8	2.5	2.6	2.5	2.3	2.3	2.3	2.1	2.3	2.2	2.2	2.3	2.3	2.1	2.3	2.2
Adjustment to school	6.1	2.6	2.9	2.8	2.3	2.5	2.4	2.3	2.4	2.4	2.2	2.3	2.3	2.2	2.3	2.3	2.5	2.6	2.6	2.6	2.6	2.6
	6.2	3.0	3.2	3.1	2.8	2.8	2.8	2.8	2.7	2.8	2.7	2.7	2.7	2.7	2.8	2.7	3.1	3.1	3.1	3.1	3.1	3.1
	6.3	3.4	3.5	3.5	3.4	3.4	3.4	3.5	3.4	3.4	3.5	3.4	3.4	3.5	3.5	3.5	3.7	3.5	3.6	3.5	3.5	3.5
	6.4	3.1	3.5	3.3	2.9	3.3	3.1	3.0	3.2	3.1	3.1	3.3	3.2	3.1	3.4	3.3	3.5	3.7	3.6	3.5	3.7	3.6
Number of schools				35			38			52			49			45			31			29

Note: the 'All' total for each year group includes pupils who have not indicated their gender.

Table 2 Pupils' average ratings of conditions in primary schools, 1999–2002

	R	Y1 Boys	Y1 Girls	Y1 All	Y2 Boys	Y2 Girls	Y2 All	Y3 Boys	Y3 Girls	Y3 All	Y4 Boys	Y4 Girls	Y4 All	Y5 Boys	Y5 Girls	Y5 All	Y6 Boys	Y6 Girls	Y6 All
	42	50	34	84	53	69	123	95	78	176	141	150	292	217	203	422	358	358	717
Thinking about my work																			
1.1	2.9	2.5	2.7	2.6	2.4	2.6	2.5	2.4	2.5	2.4	2.3	2.4	2.3	2.1	2.3	2.2	2.3	2.3	2.3
1.2	3.2	3.0	3.1	3.0	2.8	3.1	3.0	2.7	2.7	2.7	2.6	2.6	2.6	2.6	2.7	2.7	2.9	2.9	2.9
1.3	2.7	2.3	2.8	2.5	2.3	2.7	2.5	2.7	2.9	2.8	2.5	2.9	2.7	2.4	2.9	2.6	2.5	2.9	2.7
1.4	2.3	2.3	2.2	2.3	2.0	2.2	2.1	1.8	1.6	1.7	1.8	1.9	1.8	1.8	1.8	1.8	2.1	2.1	2.1
Learning by myself																			
2.1	3.2	3.4	3.5	3.5	3.4	3.5	3.5	3.3	3.4	3.3	3.3	3.5	3.4	3.4	3.4	3.4	3.5	3.6	3.5
2.2	2.5	2.6	2.7	2.6	2.8	3.1	3.0	2.7	2.9	2.8	2.6	2.7	2.6	2.5	2.5	2.5	2.8	2.9	2.9
2.3	3.0	3.3	3.3	3.3	2.9	2.9	2.9	2.7	2.6	2.6	2.5	2.7	2.6	2.5	2.5	2.5	2.3	2.3	2.3
2.4	2.3	2.0	2.6	2.3	2.3	2.5	2.4	2.1	2.0	2.1	2.2	2.3	2.3	2.0	2.2	2.1	2.4	2.6	2.5
Getting on with teachers																			
3.1	3.3	3.4	3.6	3.4	3.5	3.7	3.6	3.0	3.5	3.2	3.1	3.4	3.2	3.1	3.4	3.2	3.1	3.5	3.3
3.2	3.0	3.3	3.4	3.4	3.3	3.5	3.4	3.0	3.4	3.1	2.9	3.1	3.0	2.8	3.0	2.9	2.9	3.1	3.0
3.3	3.4	3.6	3.8	3.6	3.6	3.6	3.6	3.2	3.6	3.4	3.2	3.6	3.4	3.3	3.4	3.4	3.3	3.6	3.4
3.4	2.9	2.5	2.8	2.6	2.7	2.9	2.8	2.6	2.4	2.5	2.6	2.6	2.6	2.5	2.7	2.6	2.6	2.8	2.7
Lessons in this school																			
4.1	3.4	2.9	2.9	2.9	2.9	3.4	3.2	2.7	2.9	2.8	2.7	2.7	2.7	2.6	2.7	2.7	2.8	2.9	2.8
4.2	3.2	3.1	2.9	3.0	2.8	2.8	2.8	2.9	3.1	3.0	2.8	2.9	2.8	2.7	2.9	2.8	2.9	2.9	2.9
4.3	2.9	3.5	3.6	3.5	3.1	3.4	3.3	3.1	3.1	3.1	2.8	3.1	3.0	2.7	3.0	2.8	2.7	3.0	2.8
4.4	2.5	3.2	3.0	3.1	3.0	3.2	3.1	2.9	2.9	2.8	2.7	2.9	2.8	2.5	2.8	2.7	2.8	2.8	2.8
How I feel about my work																			
5.1	2.7	3.3	3.4	3.4	3.2	3.2	3.2	2.5	2.8	2.6	2.6	2.7	2.7	2.3	2.5	2.4	2.3	2.6	2.4
5.2	3.4	3.5	3.6	3.6	3.2	3.6	3.4	3.0	3.3	3.1	3.0	3.3	3.1	2.9	3.3	3.1	3.2	3.4	3.3
5.3	3.3	3.3	3.7	3.4	3.1	3.4	3.3	3.1	3.5	3.3	3.1	3.4	3.3	2.9	3.5	3.2	3.1	3.5	3.3
5.4	3.1	3.1	3.3	3.2	2.9	3.4	3.1	3.1	3.2	3.1	2.8	2.9	2.9	2.8	3.0	2.9	3.0	3.0	3.0
How I feel about the school rules																			
6.1	3.2	3.2	3.3	3.2	3.5	3.5	3.5	2.9	3.3	3.1	2.9	3.1	3.0	2.8	3.0	2.9	3.0	3.2	3.1
6.2	3.0	3.7	3.7	3.7	3.8	3.8	3.8	3.5	3.7	3.6	3.4	3.7	3.6	3.3	3.6	3.5	3.4	3.6	3.5
6.3	3.2	3.2	3.3	3.2	3.3	3.6	3.4	3.3	3.5	3.4	3.4	3.7	3.5	3.5	3.6	3.5	3.6	3.7	3.6
6.4	3.5	3.4	3.7	3.5	3.4	3.9	3.7	3.0	3.4	3.2	2.8	3.4	3.1	2.8	3.5	3.2	3.0	3.5	3.3
Number of schools	3			5			7			10			15			23			29

PUPIL CONDITIONS SURVEY

SECONDARY VERSION

RATING SCALE

Attached is a series of 24 statements about your school. We would like to know how far these statements match **your own** perception of the school, in other words, your **personal view** of it. There are no 'right' answers – we are seeking your opinion.

Please indicate in the boxes provided which statements reflect your personal view.

Do not put your name

BOY / GIRL (circle correct gender)

I AM IN YEAR _____

SCHOOL _____

 © *John Beresford 2003 – Creating the Conditions to Involve Pupils in Their Learning*

SELF-ASSESSMENT

1.1	At some time during the day I think about what I've learnt.			
	RARELY	SOMETIMES	OFTEN	NEARLY ALWAYS

1.2	I know how well I'm doing in school.			
	RARELY	SOMETIMES	OFTEN	NEARLY ALWAYS

1.3	I take care about what I write in any report to my parents.			
	RARELY	SOMETIMES	OFTEN	NEARLY ALWAYS

1.4	I ask teachers how I can improve my work.			
	RARELY	SOMETIMES	OFTEN	NEARLY ALWAYS

INDEPENDENT LEARNING

2.1	I can find the classroom books and equipment I need for lessons.			
	RARELY	SOMETIMES	OFTEN	NEARLY ALWAYS

2.2	We do problem solving in lessons.			
	RARELY	SOMETIMES	OFTEN	NEARLY ALWAYS

2.3	We do groupwork in lessons.			
	RARELY	SOMETIMES	OFTEN	NEARLY ALWAYS

2.4	I use books at home or in libraries to do research.			
	RARELY	SOMETIMES	OFTEN	NEARLY ALWAYS

AFFINITY TO TEACHERS

3.1	I get on well with teachers in this school.			
	RARELY	SOMETIMES	OFTEN	NEARLY ALWAYS

3.2	Teachers in this school make us want to work.			
	RARELY	SOMETIMES	OFTEN	NEARLY ALWAYS

3.3	Teachers in this school are helpful.			
	RARELY	SOMETIMES	OFTEN	NEARLY ALWAYS

3.4	We discuss with teachers what work we should do.			
	RARELY	SOMETIMES	OFTEN	NEARLY ALWAYS

LEARNING REPERTOIRE				
4.1	**Lessons in this school are varied, and don't follow a pattern.**			
	RARELY	SOMETIMES	OFTEN	NEARLY ALWAYS
4.2	**I cope with the different teaching styles that teachers use.**			
	RARELY	SOMETIMES	OFTEN	NEARLY ALWAYS
4.3	**Lessons in this school are interesting.**			
	RARELY	SOMETIMES	OFTEN	NEARLY ALWAYS
4.4	**We are taught new ways of working, for example how to work well in groups.**			
	RARELY	SOMETIMES	OFTEN	NEARLY ALWAYS

ORIENTATION TO LEARNING				
5.1	**I look forward to lessons.**			
	RARELY	SOMETIMES	OFTEN	NEARLY ALWAYS
5.2	**I work hard in school.**			
	RARELY	SOMETIMES	OFTEN	NEARLY ALWAYS
5.3	**I put lots of effort into my homework.**			
	RARELY	SOMETIMES	OFTEN	NEARLY ALWAYS
5.4	**Hard work is rewarded in this school.**			
	RARELY	SOMETIMES	OFTEN	NEARLY ALWAYS

ADJUSTMENT TO SCHOOL				
6.1	**Teachers in this school are firm but fair.**			
	RARELY	SOMETIMES	OFTEN	NEARLY ALWAYS
6.2	**I can see the sense of having school rules.**			
	RARELY	SOMETIMES	OFTEN	NEARLY ALWAYS
6.3	**My weekly attendance at school is good.**			
	RARELY	SOMETIMES	OFTEN	NEARLY ALWAYS
6.4	**My behaviour in school is good.**			
	RARELY	SOMETIMES	OFTEN	NEARLY ALWAYS

© John Beresford 2003 – Creating the Conditions to Involve Pupils in Their Learning

PUPIL CONDITIONS SURVEY

PRIMARY VERSION

RATING SCALE

Attached are 24 questions about your school. There are no right answers – we want to know **your** views about your school.

Please tick in the boxes provided which of the words – rarely, sometimes, often, nearly always – best give your own view.

Do not put your name

BOY / GIRL (circle correct gender)

I AM IN YEAR _____

SCHOOL _____

THINKING ABOUT MY WORK			

1.1	At some time in each school day do you think about what you've been learning at school?		
	RARELY	SOMETIMES	OFTEN	NEARLY ALWAYS

1.2	Do you know when you've done something well in school?		
	RARELY	SOMETIMES	OFTEN	NEARLY ALWAYS

1.3	Do you talk about what you've been doing at school to people at home?		
	RARELY	SOMETIMES	OFTEN	NEARLY ALWAYS

1.4	Do you ask your teacher how you can improve your work?		
	RARELY	SOMETIMES	OFTEN	NEARLY ALWAYS

LEARNING BY MYSELF			

2.1	Can you find the books and equipment that you need for your work in the classroom?		
	RARELY	SOMETIMES	OFTEN	NEARLY ALWAYS

2.2	Are you asked to find out things for yourself and solve problems in lessons?		
	RARELY	SOMETIMES	OFTEN	NEARLY ALWAYS

2.3	Do you work in groups in lessons?		
	RARELY	SOMETIMES	OFTEN	NEARLY ALWAYS

2.4	Do you use books at home to help you with your work?		
	RARELY	SOMETIMES	OFTEN	NEARLY ALWAYS

GETTING ON WITH TEACHERS			

3.1	Do you get on well with the teachers in this school?		
	RARELY	SOMETIMES	OFTEN	NEARLY ALWAYS

3.2	Does your teacher make things interesting and exciting which make you want to work?		
	RARELY	SOMETIMES	OFTEN	NEARLY ALWAYS

3.3	Is your teacher helpful?		
	RARELY	SOMETIMES	OFTEN	NEARLY ALWAYS

3.4	Do you talk to your teacher about the work you have to do?		
	RARELY	SOMETIMES	OFTEN	NEARLY ALWAYS

© John Beresford 2003 – Creating the Conditions to Involve Pupils in Their Learning

LESSONS IN THIS SCHOOL				
4.1	Are the lessons varied? Are your lessons done in different ways?			
	RARELY	SOMETIMES	OFTEN	NEARLY ALWAYS
4.2	Does your teacher use different ways of working?			
	RARELY	SOMETIMES	OFTEN	NEARLY ALWAYS
4.3	Are the lessons interesting? (Do you enjoy the lessons?)			
	RARELY	SOMETIMES	OFTEN	NEARLY ALWAYS
4.4	Are you taught new ways of working, for example how to work well in groups or with a partner?			
	RARELY	SOMETIMES	OFTEN	NEARLY ALWAYS

HOW I FEEL ABOUT MY WORK				
5.1	Do you look forward to lessons?			
	RARELY	SOMETIMES	OFTEN	NEARLY ALWAYS
5.2	Do you work hard in school?			
	RARELY	SOMETIMES	OFTEN	NEARLY ALWAYS
5.3	Do you try your best with your homework? (When you read at home etc.)			
	RARELY	SOMETIMES	OFTEN	NEARLY ALWAYS
5.4	If you work hard do you receive praise?			
	RARELY	SOMETIMES	OFTEN	NEARLY ALWAYS

HOW I FEEL ABOUT THE SCHOOL RULES				
6.1	Are the teachers firm but fair?			
	RARELY	SOMETIMES	OFTEN	NEARLY ALWAYS
6.2	Is it important to have school rules?			
	RARELY	SOMETIMES	OFTEN	NEARLY ALWAYS
6.3	Do you come to school every day?			
	RARELY	SOMETIMES	OFTEN	NEARLY ALWAYS
6.4	Is your behaviour in school good?			
	RARELY	SOMETIMES	OFTEN	NEARLY ALWAYS

References and further reading

Ainscow, M., Hopkins, D., Southworth G. and West, M. (1994) *Creating the Conditions for School Improvement*. London: David Fulton Publishers.

Ainscow, M., Beresford, J., Harris, A., Hopkins, D., Southworth, G. and West, M. (2000) *Creating the Conditions for School Improvement* (2nd edition). London: David Fulton Publishers.

Assessment Reform Group (1999) *Assessment for Learning: Beyond the Black Box*. Cambridge: The Assessment Reform Group.

Barber, M. (1996) *The Learning Game: Arguments for an Education Revolution*. London: Victor Gollancz.

Barnett, T. (1985) 'Pupil personality and styles of teaching', *Pastoral Care*, **3**(3), 207–15.

Barsby, J. (1991) 'Self-evaluation and seven year olds', *Education 3–13*, **19**(1), 12–17.

Barth, R. S. (1996) 'Building a community of learners', paper prepared for California School Leadership Center.

Beresford, J. (1995) 'Classroom conditions for school improvement: a literature review', paper prepared for ICSEI, *Learning from Each Other*, London, October.

Beresford, J. (1997) 'Improving reading: how pupils' views can help', *Reading*, **31**(3), 3–8.

Beresford, J. (1998a) *Collecting Information for School Improvement*. London: David Fulton Publishers.

Beresford, J. (1998b) 'Target Practice', *Managing Schools Today*, **7**(4), 22–5.

Beresford, J. (1999a) 'Some reflections on the conduct and reporting of inspections in England and Sweden', paper presented to ICSEI, San Antonio, January.

Beresford, J. (1999b) 'Matching teaching to learning', *The Curriculum Journal*, **10**(3), 321–44.

Beresford, J. (1999c) 'Assessment of classroom performance – by pupils?', *Improving Schools*, **2**(2), 28–9.

Beresford, J. (2002) 'Classroom conditions for school improvement: students' views', unpublished PhD thesis, University of Nottingham.

Beresford, J. (2003) 'Developing students as effective learners: the student conditions for school improvement', *School Effectiveness and School Improvement*, **14**(2), June, in press.

Beresford, J. and Payne, G. (1997) 'Generating data for school improvement – the role of the external researcher in school improvement', paper presented to BERA Conference, York, September.

Black, P. and Wiliam, D. (1998a) *Inside the Black Box*. Mimeo, King's College, London.

Black, P. and Wiliam, D. (1998b) 'Assessment and Classroom Learning', *Assessment in Education*, **5**(1), 7–75.

Black, P., Harrison, C., Lee, C., Marshall, B. and Wiliam, D. (2002) *Working Inside the Black Box*. Mimeo, King's College, London.

Blatchford, P. and Kutnick, P. (1996) 'Studying pupil groups in primary school classrooms: where is the pedagogy?', paper presented to BERA Conference, Lancaster, September.

Bleach, K. (1997) 'Raising boys' achievement', address at Cambridge Institute of Education, 9 July.

Blum, R. E. (1997) 'Learning what students think about school restructuring', in Restructuring Collaborative (1997) *Look Who's Talking Now. Student Views of Learning in Restructuring Schools.* Portland: Regional Educational Laboratory Network, Chapter 1.

Bowyer, M. (1981) 'The independent learning of a foreign language', *Forum*, **23**(2), 41–2.

Boyd, B. and Jardine, S. (1997) '"Sometimes our views get lost". Listening to young people talking about school', paper presented to BERA Conference, York, September.

Brandes, D. and Ginnis, P. (1990) *The Student-Centered School: Ideas for practical visionaries*. Oxford: Blackwell.

Brophy, J. and Good, T. L. (1986) 'Teacher behavior and student achievement', in Wittrock, M. C. (ed.) *Handbook of Research on Teaching* (3rd edition). New York: Macmillan, Chapter 12.

Brown, S. and McIntyre, D. (1993) *Making Sense of Teaching*. Buckingham: Open University Press.

Callaghan, The Right Honourable J. (1976) 'The Ruskin College Speech', in Ahier, J., Cosin, B. and Hales, M. (eds) (1996) *Diversity and Change. Education, Policy and Selection*. London: Routledge, with the Open University, Chapter 10.

Campbell, I. (1993) 'Disaffected school students', *Forum*, **35**(3), 89–90.

Campbell, R. (1986) 'Social relationships in hearing children read', *Reading*, **20**(3), 157–67.

Castelijns, J. (1996) 'Responsive instruction to enhance young children's task motivation', paper presented to BERA Conference, Lancaster, September.

Chaplain, R. (1996a) 'Pupils under pressure: coping with stress at school', in Rudduck, J., Chaplain, R. and Wallace, G. (eds) *School Improvement: What Can Pupils Tell Us?* London: David Fulton Publishers, Chapter 9.

Chaplain, R. (1996b) 'Making a strategic withdrawal: disengagement and self-worth protection in male pupils', in Rudduck, J., Chaplain, R. and Wallace, G. (eds) *School Improvement: What Can Pupils Tell Us?* London: David Fulton Publishers, Chapter 8.

Clarke, D. F. (1991) 'The Negotiated Syllabus: what is it and how is it likely to work?', *Applied Linguistics*, **12**(1), 13–28.

Cockett, M. (1996) 'Improving attendance and reducing disaffection: finding strategies which last', paper presented to BERA Conference, Lancaster, September.

Connolly, P. (1997) 'In search of authenticity: researching young children's perspectives', in Pollard, A., Thiessen, D. and Filer, A. (eds) *Children and their Curriculum. The Perspectives of Primary and Elementary School Children*. London: Falmer Press, Chapter 8.

Cooper, P. and Fielding, M. (1998) 'The issue of student voice', paper presented to ICSEI, Manchester, January.

Creemers, B. P. M. (1994) *The Effective Classroom*. London/New York: Cassell.

Crozier, G. (1999) 'School students' control over their own learning: a novel idea or radical alternative?', paper presented to BERA Conference, Brighton, September.

Cunliffe, A. (1995) 'How do my students believe they learn?', paper presented to Conference of Australian Science Teachers' Association.

Daniels, S. and Welford, G. (1990) 'Self-assessment: pleasant surprise or harsh reality?', *Evaluation and Research in Education*, **4**(1), 1–10.

Dann, R. (1996) 'Pupil self-assessment in the primary classroom. A case for action', *Education 3–13*, October, 55–9.

Day, C., Harris, A., Hadfield, M., Tolley, H. and Beresford, J. (2000) *Leading Schools in Times of Change*. Buckingham: Open University Press.

Day, J. (1996) 'The Reckoning', in Rudduck, J., Chaplain, R. and Wallace, G. (eds) *School Improvement: What Can Pupils Tell Us?* London: David Fulton Publishers, Chapter 12.

Department for Education and Employment (DfEE) (1997) *Excellence in schools. Cm 3681*. London: The Stationery Office.

Department for Education and Employment (DfEE) (2001) *Teaching and Learning in the Foundation Subjects*: www.standards.dfes.gov.uk/keystage3/strands/tlf/ (accessed December 2001).

De Pear, S. (1997) 'Excluded pupils' views of their educational needs and experiences', *Support for Learning*, **12**(1), 19–22.

Doddington, C., Flutter, J. and Rudduck, J. (1999) *Improving Learning: The Pupils' Agenda. A Report for primary schools*. Cambridge: Homerton College, April.

Elliott, J. (1997) '"Disaffected pupils": perspectives on the problem', paper presented to BERA Conference, York, September.

Elliott (Julian), Stewart-Smith, Y. and Hildreth, A. (1997) 'Attitudes to education – a three nation comparison', paper presented to BERA Conference, York, September.

Epstein, J. L. and McPartland, J. M. (1976) 'The concept and measurement of the quality of school life', *American Educational Research Journal*, **13**(1), 15–30.

Faccenda, J. and Fielding, M. (1992) *Learning Styles in FE*, Model Making Colleges Pack. Brighton: University of Sussex.

Fielding, M. (1994) 'Valuing difference in teachers and learners: building on Kolb's learning styles to develop a language of teaching and learning', *The Curriculum Journal*, **5**(3), 393–417.

Fielding, M. (1995) 'Mapping the progress of change', paper presented to BERA/ECER Conference, Bath, September.

Fielding, M. (1999) 'Target setting, policy pathology and student perspectives: learning to labour in new times', *Cambridge Journal of Education*, **29**(2), 277–87.

Fielding, M. (2001) 'Students as radical agents of change'. Mimeo, University of Sussex Institute of Education.

Flutter, J., Rudduck, J., Addams, H., Johnson, M. and Maden, M. (1999) *Improving Learning: The Pupils' Agenda. A report for secondary schools*. Cambridge: Homerton College, April.

Galloway, D., Leo, E., Rogers, C. and Armstrong, D. (1995) 'Motivational styles in English and mathematics among children identified as having special educational needs', *British Journal of Educational Psychology*, 65, 477–87.

Gibbs, S. E. (1989) 'The final frontier. Independent learning and the role of the library', *School Librarian*, **37**(1), 10–11.

Giddens, A. (1990) *The Consequences of Modernity*. Oxford: Polity Press.

Gipps, C. (1992) *What We Know About Effective Primary Teaching*. London: The Tufnell Press.

Gipps, C. and Tunstall, P. (1997) 'Effort, ability and the teacher: young children's explanations for success and failure', paper presented to BERA Conference, York, September.

Gonzalez, G. and Gilbert, J. (1980) '"A" Level physics by the use of an independent learning approach: the role of the lab-work', *British Educational Research Journal*, **6**(1), 63–83.

Gracie, M. (1981) 'Closely observed children', *Forum*, **23**(2), p. 42–4.

Hacker, R. G. and Carter, D. S. G. (1987) 'Teaching processes in social studies classrooms and prescriptive instructional theories', *British Educational Research Journal*, **13**(3), 261–9.

Hansen, D. T. (1993) 'The moral importance of the teacher's style', *Journal of Curriculum Studies*, **25**(5), 397–421.

Hargreaves, D. H. (2001) 'A capital theory of school effectiveness and improvement [1]', *British Educational Research Journal*, **27**(4), 487–503.

Haroun, R. and O'Hanlon, C. (1997) 'Do teachers and students agree in their perception of what school discipline is?', *Educational Review*, **49**(3), 237–50.

Harris, A. (1995) 'Effective teaching', *SIN Research Matters*, 3 (Summer). London Institute of Education.

Harris, A. (2002) *Leading the Improving Department*. London: David Fulton Publishers.

Haviland, J. (ed.) (1988) *Take Care, Mr Baker!* London: Fourth Estate.

Hayes, D. (1993) 'The Good, The Bad, The Ugly and The Memorable: A retrospective view of teacher-pupil relationships', *Education 3–13*, **21**(1), 53–9.

Hayes, L. F. and Ross, D. D. (1989) 'Trust versus control: the impact of school leadership on teacher reflection', *International Journal of Qualitative Studies in Education*, **2**(4), 335–50.

Hazelwood, R. D., Fitz-Gibbon, C. and McCabe, C. (1988) 'Student perception of teaching and learning styles in TVEI', *Evaluation and Research in Education*, **2**(2), 61–8.

Hickey, C. and Fitzclarence, L. (1999) 'Peering at the individual: problems with trying to teach young males not to be like their peers', paper presented to BERA Conference, Brighton, September.

Homerton-Schools Research Circle (1997) 'Making your way through secondary school', Research Briefing. Series 1, Number 2.

Homerton-Schools Research Circle (1999) 'The Challenge of Year 8', Research Briefing. Series 2, Number 3.

Hopkins, D. (2001) *Meeting the Challenge*. Nottingham: DfEE Standards and Effectiveness Unit.

Hopkins, D. (2002) *Improving the Quality of Education for All*. London: David Fulton Publishers.

Hopkins, D., West, M. and Beresford, J. (1995) 'Creating the Conditions for Classroom Improvement. An interim report', paper delivered to ECER, Bath, September.

Hopkins, D., West, M. and Ainscow, M. (1996) *Improving the Quality of Education for All: Progress and Challenge*. London: David Fulton Publishers.

Hopkins, D., West, M., Ainscow, M., Harris, A. and Beresford, J. (1997) *Creating the conditions for classroom improvement*. London: David Fulton Publishers.

Hopkins, D., West, M. and Beresford, J. (1998) 'Creating the conditions for classroom and teacher development', *Teachers and Teaching: theory and practice*, **4**(1), 115–41.

Hopkins, D. and Harris, A. (2000) *Creating the Conditions for Teaching and Learning*. London: David Fulton Publishers.

Hord, S. M. (1997) 'Speaking with high school students in the southwest', in Restructuring Collaborative (1997) *Look Who's Talking Now. Student Views of Learning in Restructuring Schools*. Portland: Regional Educational Laboratory Network, Chapter 4.

Hubbard, G. (1997) 'Pupil-managed co-operative learning: why and how pupils interact and co-operate', paper presented to BERA Conference, York, September.

Hughes, P. (1994) 'Implications for curriculum reform from OECD associated projects', in OECD (1994) *The Curriculum Redefined: Schooling for the 21st Century*. Paris: OECD, Paper 13.

Hughes, P. and Skilbeck M. (1994) 'Curriculum reform – recent trends and issues', in OECD (1994) *The Curriculum Redefined: Schooling for the 21st Century*. Paris: OECD, Paper 1.

Jackson, D., Raymond, L., Weatherill, L. and Fielding, M. (1998) 'Students as researchers', paper presented to ICSEI, Manchester, January.

Joyce, B. and Weil, M. (1986) *Models of Teaching* (3rd edition). Englewood Cliffs, NJ: Prentice Hall.

Joyce, B., Showers, B. and Rolheiser-Bennett, C. (1987) 'Staff development and student learning: a synthesis of research on models of teaching', *Educational Leadership*, **45**(2), 11–23.

Joyce, B., Calhoun, E. and Hopkins, D. (1997) *Models of Learning – Tools for Teaching*. Buckingham: Open University Press.

Kaminski, F. (1999) 'Semi-independent learning: an approach to mixed-ability grouping – a case study', *Forum*, **41**(2), 78–82.

Kershner, R. (1996) 'The meaning of "working hard" in school', in Rudduck, J., Chaplain, R. and Wallace, G. (eds) *School Improvement: What Can Pupils Tell Us?* London: David Fulton Publishers, Chapter 6.

Keys, W. and Fernandes, C. (1993) *What Do Students Think About School?* Slough: NFER.

King Harold School with University of Cambridge Institute of Education (1995) *'Effective Teaching for Effective Learning' Handbook.* Cambridge: Cambridge Institute of Education.

Kolb, D. A. (1984) *Experiential Learning. Experience as the Source of Learning and Development.* Englewood Cliffs, NJ: Prentice Hall.

Kyriacou, C. (1998) *Essential Teaching Skills* (2nd edition). Cheltenham: Stanley Thornes (Publishers) Ltd.

Labour Party (1995) *Excellence for Everyone. Labour's crusade to raise standards.* London: Labour Party.

Labour Party (1997) *New Labour. Because Britain Deserves Better.* London: Labour Party.

Lahelma, E., Hakala, K., Hynninen, P. and Lappalainen, S. (1999) '"We have far too few men!" Analysing the discussion on the need for more male teachers', paper presented to ECER, Lahti, September.

Levin, B. (1994) 'Improving educational productivity. Putting students at the center', *Phi Delta Kappan*, **75**(10), 758–60.

Levin, B. (1995) 'Improving educational productivity through a focus on learners', *Studies in Educational Administration*, **60**, 15–21.

Maden, M. and Johnson, M. (1998) 'Pupil attitude surveys – shedding light on dark corners', paper presented to ICSEI, Manchester, January.

Maden, M. and Rudduck, J. (1997) 'Listen to the learners', *Times Educational Supplement*, 4 July.

Marzano, R. J., Arredondo, D. E., Brandt, R. S., Pickering, D. J., Blackburn, G. J. and Moffett, C. A. (1992) *Dimensions of Learning.* Teacher's Manual. Aurora, CO: ASCD/McREL Institute.

McLean, M. (1990) 'School knowledge traditions', in Ahier, J., Cosin, B. and Hales, M. (eds) *Diversity and Change. Education, Policy and Selection.* London: Routledge, with the Open University, Chapter 2.

Meece, J. L. and Miller, S. D. (1996) 'Developmental changes in children's self-reports of achievement goals, competence, and strategy use during the late elementary years', paper presented to AERA Conference, New York, April.

Miller, D., Parkhouse, P., Eagle, R. and Evans, T. (1999) 'Pupils and the core subjects: a study of the attitudes of some pupils aged 11–16', paper presented to BERA Conference, Brighton, September.

Morgan, C. and Morris, G. (1999) *Good Teaching and Learning: Pupils and Teachers Speak.* Buckingham: Open University Press.

MORI/Campaign For Learning (1998) *Attitudes to Learning '98.* London: Campaign For Learning.

Mortimore, P., Sammons, P., Stoll, L., Lewis, D. and Ecob, R. (1988) *School Matters. The Junior Years* (2nd edition). London: Paul Chapman Publishing.

Munn, P., Johnstone, M. and Holligan, C. (1990) 'Pupils' perceptions of "effective disciplinarians"', *British Educational Research Journal*, **16**(2), 191–8.

Newton, P. and Harwood, D. (1993) 'Teaching styles and personal and social education: how far have "active learning" strategies permeated the secondary curriculum?', *Pastoral Care*, **11**(1), 36–42.

Nisbet, J. (1994) 'Relating pupil assessment and evaluation to teaching and learning', in OECD, *The Curriculum Redefined: Schooling for the 21st Century.* Paris. OECD, Paper 14.

Norwich, B. (1998) 'Developing an inventory of children's class learning approaches', *Educational Psychology in Practice*, **14**(3), 147–55.

Office for Standards in Education (Ofsted) (1999) *Handbook for Inspecting Primary and Nursery Schools*. London: The Stationery Office.

Organization for Economic Cooperation and Development (OECD) (1994) *The Curriculum Redefined: Schooling for the 21st Century*. Paris: OECD.

Osborn, M. (1997a) 'When being top is not seen as best', *Times Educational Supplement*, 10 January, p. 14.

Osborn, M. (1997b) 'Learning, working and climbing the ladder: pupil perspectives on primary schooling in England and France', paper presented to ECER, Frankfurt-am-Main, January.

Osborne, J. and Collins, S. (1999) 'Pupils' and parents' views of the role and value of the science curriculum', paper presented to BERA Conference, Brighton, September.

Parker-Rees, R. (1997) 'The tale of a task: learning beyond the map', in Pollard, A., Thiessen, D. and Filer, A. (eds) *Children and their Curriculum. The Perspectives of Primary and Elementary School Children*. London: Falmer Press, Chapter 2.

Perkins, P. (1999) 'Mini-targets: an approach to target setting', *Improving Schools*, **2**(1), 16–17.

Phillimore, A. J. (1989) 'Flexible specialization, work organization and skills', in Ahier, J., Cosin, B. and Hales, M. (eds) (1996) *Diversity and Change. Education, Policy and Selection*. London: Routledge, with the Open University, Chapter 6.

Qualifications and Curriculum Authority (QCA) (2000) *Key Skills*: www.qca.org.uk (accessed December 2001).

Raynor, D. (1995) 'Identifying trends in pupil self-assessment at different ability levels', *Pastoral Care*, June, 29–31.

Restructuring Collaborative (1997) *Look Who's Talking Now. Student Views of Learning in Restructuring Schools*. Portland: Regional Educational Laboratory Network.

Rosenshine, B. and Stevens, R. (1986) 'Teaching functions', in Wittrock, M. C. (ed.) *Handbook of Research on Teaching* (3rd edition). New York: Macmillan, Chapter 13.

Rudduck, J. (1995) 'What can pupils tell us about School Improvement?', paper presented to ICSEI, London, October.

Rudduck, J. (1996a) 'Getting serious: the demands of coursework, revision and examinations', in Rudduck, J., Chaplain, R. and Wallace, G. (eds) *School Improvement: What Can Pupils Tell Us?* London: David Fulton Publishers, Chapter 10.

Rudduck, J. (1996b) 'Lessons, subjects and the curriculum: issues of "understanding" and "coherence"', in Rudduck, J., Chaplain, R. and Wallace, G. (eds) *School Improvement: What Can Pupils Tell Us?* London: David Fulton Publishers, Chapter 4.

Rudduck, J. (1998) 'Consulting students as key witnesses in school improvement: how radical is their advice?', paper presented to ICSEI, Manchester, January.

Rudduck, J., Chaplain, R. and Wallace, G. (1996a) 'Pupil voices and school improvement', in Rudduck, J., Chaplain, R. and Wallace, G. (eds) *School*

Improvement: What Can Pupils Tell Us? London: David Fulton Publishers, Chapter 1.

Rudduck, J., Chaplain, R. and Wallace, G. (1996b) 'Reviewing the conditions of learning in school', in Rudduck, J., Chaplain, R. and Wallace, G. (eds) *School Improvement: What Can Pupils Tell Us?* London: David Fulton Publishers, Chapter 13.

Rudduck, J. and Flutter, J. (1998) *The Dilemmas and Challenges of Year 8.* Cambridge: Homerton College.

Rudduck, J. and Flutter, J. (2000) 'Pupil participation and pupil perspective: "carving a new order of experience"', *Cambridge Journal of Education,* **30**(1), 75–89.

Rutter, M., Maughan, B., Mortimore, P. and Ouston, J. (1979) *Fifteen Thousand Hours.* London: Open Books.

Sammons, P., Hillman, J. and Mortimore, P. (1995) *Key Characteristics of Effective Schools. A review of school effectiveness research.* London: Ofsted.

Sarason, S. B. (1990) *The Predictable Failure of Educational Reform.* San Francisco: Jossey-Bass Publishers.

Scottish Consultative Council on the Curriculum (Scottish CCC) (1996) *Teaching for Effective Learning.* Dundee: Scottish CCC.

Sharnbrook Upper School (1995) *Sharnbrook Learning Project. Report of Phase 1.* Bedford: Sharnbrook Upper School.

Shaughnessy, J. and Kushman, J. W. (1997) 'Research in the hands of students', in Restructuring Collaborative (1997), *Look Who's Talking Now. Student Views of Learning in Restructuring Schools.* Portland: Regional Educational Laboratory Network, Chapter 3.

Skilbeck, M. (1994) 'The core curriculum', in OECD, *The Curriculum Redefined: Schooling in the 21st Century.* Paris: OECD, Paper 7.

Slavin, R. E. (1993) 'Co-operative learning in OECD countries: research, practice and prevalence', paper for Centre for Educational Research and Innovation, OECD, September.

Smees, R. and Thomas, S. (1998) 'Valuing pupils' views about school', *British Journal of Curriculum and Assessment,* **8**(3), 7–9.

Smith, M. (1994) 'An agenda for reform in the USA', in OECD, *The Curriculum Redefined: Schooling in the 21st Century.* Paris: OECD, Paper 2.

Southworth, G. (1998) 'The learning school: what does it look like?', *Managing Schools Today,* **7**(4), 29–30.

Spaulding, A. (1997) 'The politics of primaries: the micropolitical perspectives of 7-year-olds', in Pollard, A., Thiessen, D. and Filer, A. (eds) *Children and their Curriculum. The Perspectives of Primary and Elementary School Children.* London: The Falmer Press, Chapter 5.

Stokes, H. (1999) 'IQEA under the spotlight', *IQEA 1* (May), 2–3.

Sutcliffe, J. (1998) 'Age weakens thirst for knowledge', *Times Educational Supplement,* 22 May.

Testerman, J. (1996) 'Holding at-risk students', *Phi Delta Kappan,* **77**(5), 364–5, January.

Thiessen, D. (1997) 'Knowing about, acting on behalf of, and working with primary pupils' perspectives: three levels of engagement with research', in Pollard, A., Thiessen, D. and Filer, A. (eds) *Children and their Curriculum. The Perspectives of Primary and Elementary School Children.* London: The Falmer Press, Chapter 9.

Thiessen, D. (1998) 'Working with primary pupils' perspectives to transform schools', paper presented at ICSEI, Manchester, January.

Towler, L. and Broadfoot, P. (1992) 'Self-assessment in the primary school', *Educational Review*, **44**(2), 137–51.

Van Velzen, W., Miles, M., Ekholm, M., Hameyer, U. and Robin, D. (1985) *Making School Improvement Work: A Conceptual Guide to Practice*, Leuven, Belgium: ACCO.

Wallace, G. (1996a) 'Engaging with learning', in Rudduck, J., Chaplain, R. and Wallace, G. (eds) *School Improvement: What Can Pupils Tell Us?* London: David Fulton Publishers, Chapter 5.

Wallace, G. (1996b) 'Relating to teachers', in Rudduck, J., Chaplain, R. and Wallace, G. (eds) *School Improvement: What Can Pupils Tell Us?* London: David Fulton Publishers, Chapter 3.

Wang, M. C., Haertel, G. D. and Walberg, H. J. (1993) 'Toward a knowledge base for school learning', *Review of Educational Research*, **63**(3), 249–94.

Warrington, M. and Younger, M. (1996) 'Homework: dilemmas and difficulties', in Rudduck, J., Chaplain, R. and Wallace, G. (eds) *School Improvement: What Can Pupils Tell Us?* London: David Fulton Publishers, Chapter 7.

West, M., Hopkins, D. and Beresford, J. (1995) 'Conditions for school and classroom development', paper presented to ECER, Bath, September.

West, M. and Beresford, J. (1998) 'Issues of equity and diversity in classrooms: some of the problems confronting school improvement programmes', paper presented to ICSEI, Manchester, January.

Winston, J. (1992) 'Jackie, Eric and Me: a case study in professional development within the context of day to day school relationships', *Curriculum*, **13**(2), 110–17.

Wragg, E. (1997) 'Countdown to the new millennium', *Guardian Education*, 8 April.

Yaakobi, D. and Sharan, S. (1985) 'Teacher beliefs and practices: the discipline carries the message', *Journal of Education for Teaching*, **11**(2), 187–99.

Yamagiwa, T. (1994) 'New trends in the revised curricula in Japan', in OECD, *The Curriculum Redefined: Schooling in the 21st Century*. Paris: OECD, Paper 5.

Young, M. (1993) 'A curriculum for the twenty-first century? Towards a new basis for overcoming academic/vocational divisions', in Ahier, J., Cosin, B. and Hales, M. (eds), (1996) *Diversity and Change. Education, Policy and Selection*. London: Routledge, with the Open University, Chapter 5.

Index

IQEA 1, 2, 3, 5, 12, 13, 14, 24, 25, 38, 41, 43, 53, 69, 70, 81, 93, 94, 97, 98, 100

Joyce, B. 69

Key Skills Strategy 10
Key Stage 3 Strategy 8, 69, 96

learning autonomy 6, 9, 10, 24, 25, 50, 83
learning capacity 2, 3, 4, 5, 8, 10, 54, 63, 88, 95
learning preferences 54
learning repertoire 6, 10, 11, 53–68, 93, 96, 101
learning strategies/styles 9, 10, 24, 25, 53, 55, 57, 65
lesson plans 25, 63
lesson review 15, 16
library skills 25, 39
lifelong learning 2, 7, 9, 38, 50, 71
literacy skills 41

management capacity 95
mapping lessons 26, 27
marking 78
misbehaviour 91
motivation 9, 12, 13, 42, 45, 56, 69, 72

National Curriculum 5, 7, 42, 96, 97
note-taking 25, 38, 39, 58, 59

orientation to learning 6, 8, 11, 69–80, 102

paired work 10, 54, 58, 59
parents 2, 14, 19, 20, 21, 22, 25, 49, 101
pedagogic partnerships 6, 69
peer coaching 23, 69
planning 4, 5, 11, 17
planning for teaching 6, 24, 71
practical work 25
problem-solving 10, 11, 24, 25, 26, 29, 30, 58, 59, 101
professional relationships 1, 6
PTAs 20, 21
punishments 13
pupil mentoring 13
Pupil Voice conference 94

pupils as researchers 94

reflection 6, 11, 12, 14, 15, 19, 101
reports 19, 20
revision 49, 76
reward system 13, 17, 70, 78
rules 6, 81, 82, 85, 86, 87, 91, 92, 97, 101

schemes of work 25
school council 20, 21, 90, 93
school effectiveness 2, 3
school improvement 2, 3, 4, 5, 41, 94, 95, 98, 100
seating arrangements 23
self-assessment 6, 10, 11, 12–23, 35, 74, 101, 102
self-esteem 9, 13, 70
self-motivation 6, 8
self-reporting 19
semi-independent learning 25
social skills 31, 65
special educational needs 82
special needs pupils 13
staff development 4, 69
staff meetings 21
starts of lessons 15
summative and formative assessment 17

target-setting/targets 13, 17, 70, 82
teacher–pupil relationships 8
teaching capacity 2, 3, 4, 95
teaching and learning styles 53, 55
teaching styles/models and strategies 2, 6, 9, 10, 12, 15, 53–58, 70
teaching repertoire 1, 6, 10, 11, 53, 101
teamwork 7
technology 7, 29
Thiessen, D. 93
'traffic lighting' 22, 23
truancy 88
tutorial periods 21

VAK 53 (visual/auditory/ kinaesthetic)

white-board 23
Working inside the Black Box 22

Year 8 'dip' 69

S39987
DH

371.
3
BER

5000488907

owl